HEALTH, MONEY, and LOVE

Health, Money, and Love

. . . And Why We Don't Enjoy Them

by Robert Farrar Capon

WILLIAM B. EERDMANS PUBLISHING COMPANY
GRAND RAPIDS, MICHIGAN

Copyright © 1990 by Wm. B. Eerdmans Publishing Co.
255 Jefferson Ave. S.E., Grand Rapids, Mich. 49503

Printed in the United States of America

Library of Congress Cataloging-in-Publication Data

Capon, Robert Farrar.
    Health, money, and love—and why we don't enjoy them /
    by Robert Farrar Capon.
            p.   cm.
    ISBN 0-8028-3657-7
    1. Spiritual life—Anglican authors. 2. Happiness—Religious
    aspects—Christianity. 3. Health—Religious aspects—Christianity.
    4. Wealth—Religious aspects—Christianity. 5. Love—Religious
    aspects—Christianity. 6. God—worship and love. 7. Desire for God. I. Title.
    BV4501.2.C265   1990
    248.4—dc20   90-41600
                                                            CIP

Contents

THE PURSUIT OF HAPPINESS

1
MOVIE   3

2
DIALOGUE   12

3
INTERLUDE   26

4
STORY   41

v

THE COURSE OF THE PURSUIT

5
CHILDHOOD   59

6
CHILDHOOD: MORE   73

7
ROMANCE   99

8
ROMANCE: FURTHER   124

9
VOCATION   139

10
WELL-BEING   154

11
POSTSCRIPT   165

12
EPILOGUE   176

THE PURSUIT OF HAPPINESS

Some Entertainment at the Outset

1

Movie

LET ME BEGIN IN THE MIDDLE OF THE SUBJECT — WITH A STORY.

Once upon a time, there lived a king who was rich beyond the dreams of other kings. He had twelve castles (one for each month of the year), he dined sumptuously every day, and he owned the world's largest collection of obsolete corkscrews. Yet despite the number of things that filled his world, he was not as happy as kings are supposed to be.

For one thing, he worried about his health: too many colds in the winter, shortness of breath on the stairs, bigger love handles than he thought becoming—that sort of thing. As a man of forty-five he was beginning to find it depressing to wake up every morning feeling like a man of forty-five.

He also worried about money: it never delivered what it promised. Not that he couldn't buy anything he wanted; just that he never particularly wanted anything after he bought it. He tried carrying cash in the hope that he could get a kick out of springing for other people's bar tabs, but it just embarrassed them. Not even impulse buying cheered him up: recently he picked up a dozen boxes of Mallomars in an out-of-the-way country store; but the chocolate wasn't as good as he remembered and half the boxes were stale.

Most of all, though, he worried about love—or more accurately, about not being loved enough, which is the way most people, kings or not, worry about it. His wife, the queen, spent her days taking tea or judging farm produce and her evenings blaming him for not paying more attention to her. He in turn blamed her for being both castrating and correct; and their children blamed the two of them for not creating a happy home. Like everyone else, he had been raised to believe that love was the key to happiness. Lately, however, he had decided that love was in fact a skeleton key: it opened not only the door of happiness but all the other doors in the house, most of which took you into rooms filled with either resentment or routine.

Happiness, of course, was supposedly still somewhere on the premises. But what it was doing—whether it was in the basement building harpsichords, in the den reading Proust, or up in the attic lying bound and gagged; and what it wanted of him—whether it wished to be left alone, or to be brought a Cognac, or to be rescued from its captivity; and what his chances were of finding the right room even if he knew the answers to all of the above—he had no idea and no interest whatsoever. But only for one minute more. For in his castle there lived a young and beautiful parlormaid . . .

Enough background, though. Let me give you the rest of the story of *The King and the Parlormaid* in the movie version.

INTERIOR CASTLE—NIGHT

We FADE IN on some almost burned-out embers in the main fireplace of the king's chambers. We SEE two royally shod feet appear before the fireplace and we HOLD FOR SEVERAL BEATS as we watch a poker being applied to the fire with negative results.

*CLOSE ON THE POKER as it is put back in its holder; then REVERSE
ON THE KING as he goes to his seat opposite the fireplace. HE SITS,
and we SEE on his face a look that is part boredom and part anger. He
sighs, and immediately there is a knock at the door. We HOLD SEVERAL
BEATS ON THE KING as he makes no response. The knock is repeated,
and during the following exchange, we SEE his look soften and a flicker
of interest appear on his face.*

KING   *(annoyed)*

Come! . . . Come!

ON PARLORMAID as she enters.

*KING'S POINT OF VIEW: We SEE a beautiful girl in her late twenties
carrying a tray with flatware, glassware, wine, and six covered silver
dishes. She is perfectly calm—self-possessed, but with no need to prove it.*

We HOLD A BEAT on her and then REVERSE ON THE KING.

KING   *(his annoyance partially suppressed)*

Dinner? Already? What time is it?

CROSS-CUTTING BETWEEN THEM:

PARLORMAID

Quarter past eight, your Majesty.

KING

Well, that makes it too early to be hungry and too late to digest all
that haute cuisine. What examples of the chef's ego trips have you
got there anyway? Lobster medallions in aspic, I suppose? Ragoût
of venison? Salmi of pheasant? With an entire *Reine de Saba*, no
doubt, to pack it all down tight.

PARLORMAID *(with a slight but conspiratorial smile)*

Shall I take it away then, your Majesty?

KING *(brightening)*

No. Set it down over here and let's see exactly how he's plotted to destroy yet another night's sleep.

> *MEDIUM SHOT as the girl puts the tray on a table across from the king's chair. We SEE the king walk over to the table and stand next to her. CLOSE ON THE KING'S HANDS as he begins uncovering the dishes one by one. We SEE that they are all identical, and covered with potato chips. REVERSE ON THE KING'S FACE. We SEE him at first nonplussed, then suddenly aware of what has happened.*

KING *(finally addressing the girl rather than talking mostly to himself)*

Hmm. Tell me. How would you suppose that *these* got here?

> *ON THE PARLORMAID as we SEE her smile broaden slightly:*

PARLORMAID

I would think, Sir, that there was a mix-up in the kitchen, and that I was given the tray intended for the servants' supper by mistake.

> *ON THE KING, now definitely enjoying himself:*

KING

Yes. Quite. But how then do you explain the wine? Do the servants habitually drink my best Montrachet with their . . . what *are* these things anyway?

> *We HOLD ON THE KING during the next sentence, then CUT TO THE GIRL.*

PARLORMAID

Tuna-noodle Surprises, your Majesty. But very good. The chef uses the best Cheddar and just a hint of Worcestershire.

> *ON THE PARLORMAID as the king continues.*

KING

Intriguing. And do we next suppose that the servants are at this moment condemned to washing down their regal dinner with that dreadful shipper's Muscadet I've been putting up with recently?

> *At the King's use of "we" we SEE that the girl has noticed his inclusion of her but is unflustered by it.*

PARLORMAID

I would think so, Sir.

> *CROSS-CUTTING BETWEEN THEM:*

KING

Well then. Tell me one last thing. Do you have any pressing duties at the moment?

PARLORMAID

Not if you say so, Sir.

KING *(now completely brightened)*

Excellent! Then I say so. I tell you what we shall do. You and I are going to sit down and teach them a lesson. We shall bravely dispose of these Tuna-noodle Surprises with Montrachet and then have a nice long chat while they quake in their boots over the mix-up. And after that, we shall say nothing about it, ever. How does that strike you? And by the way: if we're going to eat together, you may dispense with all the "Sirs" and "your Majestys."

ON PARLORMAID as she smiles broadly. She makes a slight curtsy, and we SEE that she intends it more as an acceptance of his overtures than as routine deference.

PARLORMAID

I think I would like that very much.

KING

Good. Then let's get on with it.

WIDER SHOT—The girl goes to a sideboard for another place setting and she and the king arrange the dinner on the table. As he helps her into her chair we SEE HIS HAND rest momentarily on her waist. We SEE them begin to eat as MUSIC comes up softly. Though we do not catch many words, we HEAR their conversation become more animated. From time to time we SEE the king reach out and lay his hand on hers. We DISSOLVE to the end of the meal, and we SEE the girl reach out and take the king's hand.

CLOSE ON HANDS—their fingers intertwine and we SEE them stand, slowly move toward each other, embrace, and kiss.

MUSIC COMES UP, and we DISSOLVE TO:

INTERIOR KING'S PRIVATE BEDCHAMBER—LATER THE SAME NIGHT

We SEE the king and the girl in bed, holding each other close after having made love.

CLOSE ON THE TWO OF THEM:

KING *(speaking softly but feelingly)*

It's been a long time since that's been even possible.

PARLORMAID

I would never have suspected.

KING

No. I mean it. It's you, you know: you make me alive. Listen. I know this is going to sound like something I say to parlormaids six times a week, but it's not. I love you. Maybe it's crazy, but I do.

PARLORMAID

It's not crazy. I know how you feel. I've loved you ever since I came here a year ago, but I never thought anything could come of it.

>*(she kisses him)*

It was a wonderful gift.

KING *(sitting up suddenly)*

Why do you say "was"?

PARLORMAID

Because nothing more is possible for us.

KING

What if we could make it possible?

PARLORMAID

But how . . . ?

KING *(lying down beside her again)*

Look. I could say something royal, like "I'll make it happen," but that would be stupid. All I know is that the most important thing in my life—which is you and me—has happened already, and no matter what we try to do to call it off, it will just go on happening. So why fight it?

PARLORMAID

But . . .

KING

No buts. Don't you understand? You said it first, for heaven's sake: we've already turned into an *us*. And if that's a fact, then somehow we have to make a life together. I haven't the foggiest notion how it will work out, but we're not going to let it slip by without trying. For openers, you're going to bring me breakfast, lunch, and dinner, plus afternoon tea every day, indefinitely. Then we'll see about the rest.

PARLORMAID

Isn't that going to be a bit . . . difficult?

> *MUSIC UP*

KING

Of course. But nowhere near as difficult as what I've been doing before tonight. Look. I love you. That's that. The rest is just a matter of doing something with both hands for a change. Are you with me?

PARLORMAID *(as she rolls over and kisses him)*

Yes . . . Yes. I love you. And you're right: that's that.

MEDIUM SHOT as they begin to make love again; MUSIC COMES UP dramatically as we HOLD on the scene. Then, as MUSIC FADES TO SILENCE we DISSOLVE TO:

INTERIOR VESTIBULE OF KING'S CHAMBERS—MUCH LATER THE SAME NIGHT

We SEE the king and the girl walking silently hand in hand toward the doorway. As they reach the door, MUSIC COMES UP AGAIN softly. We SEE them hold each other in a long embrace and kiss quietly. The girl takes the king's hand as she begins to exit the doorway.

CLOSE ON JOINED HANDS:

FREEZE FRAME:

SUPERIMPOSE:

And they lived happily ever after.

It is THE END.

2

Dialogue

NOW THEN. WE NEED TO TALK.

Unless I'm mistaken, the longer you think about that story, the less you like it. What seemed in the telling like a lighthearted bit of cinematic fluff now strikes you as either trifling or outrageous. In any case, you are just itching to put me on the witness stand and cross-examine me on the suspect testimony of my story. You want, in short, to have my hide.

Fair enough. You shall have your day in court. But to give our proceedings a less forensic tone, let us set them up as an old-fashioned reader/author dialogue with you as *Lector* and me as *Auctor*—and perhaps with the ghost of Hilaire Belloc (who loved this sort of thing) as our judge. If that's agreeable, why don't you go first?

Lector: Thank you. I do indeed have objections to your story, but before I get to them, I have a question: What on earth does this tale of dalliance among the idle rich have to do with the topics of health, money, and love as announced in your title? And in particular, what can it possibly have to do with the lives of ordinary, un-idle, un-rich people—for whom, presumably, you are writing this book?

Auctor: At the moment, nothing; eventually, everything.

Lector: Please do not be cryptic; I have an allergy to veiled utterance.

Auctor: Forgive me. It's just that my story has to do with happiness (the major subject of which health, money, and love are subtopics), and that we cannot talk about any of these things until we have first dealt with your profoundly confused attitude toward happiness itself.

Lector: With *my* confused attitude?! That's preposterous. You hardly know me.

Auctor: I hardly need to. The entire human race is confused on the subject. We're all in this together.

Lector: Perhaps. But I'm still not sure I like your drift. You hand me a lamely told tale written in a mishmash of styles. You make me sit still through the antics of two self-indulgent opportunists whose example is an open invitation to irresponsibility. You paste over them at the end a totally unlikely "they lived happily ever after." And then you have the nerve to fault my attitude?

Auctor: As I said, I fault my own as well.

Lector: I do not pretend to know about yours; my attitude toward happiness is just fine: I approve of it heartily and I pursue it energetically.

Auctor: I think you will find that your pursuit is more energetic than your approval is hearty.

Lector: Please! Remember my allergy. One more of those and I'll get a rash.

Auctor: Sorry. Let me be plain, then. You *don't* approve of happiness—and I can prove it.

Lector: How?

Auctor: By every word you have said so far. I gave you a love story with a happy ending. But what have you done with it? You have picked and carped about lameness, about mishmash of styles, about self-indulgence, about irresponsibility, and about total unlikeliness. I feel like a first-grader who has brought home a happy drawing with a bright yellow sun in the sky: you're the Daddy who insists on faulting the details rather than looking at the picture. Why?

Lector: Because you're not a first-grader; you ought to know better.

Auctor: Ah! Not so fast. You have two resounding clunkers in there that I simply can't let pass.

Lector: Clunkers? Two?

Auctor: Absolutely. The first is the old, "I'm going to correct you until you stop embarrassing me in front of my friends" ploy. The Daddy of the first-grader probably began by telling his child, "You're not a kindergartener"—his implication being that it's time for the kid to cut out this immature nonsense about happy pictures and get down to Drawing By The Rules so Daddy can be proud of him at the PTA art show.

Lector:　But I didn't mean . . .

Auctor:　But you did. My story was annoying and embarrassing
to you; but rather than face the source of your embarrassment,
you took exception to all the things you found wrong with my
telling of it. Which brings me to the second clunker, namely,
your statement that I ought to know better. Better than what,
may I ask?

Lector:　Better than to have a king and a parlormaid fall deeply
and permanently in love and then have them get away with a
successful, undiscovered, lifelong adultery right under the noses
of everyone else in their lives.

Auctor:　Tell me something. What exactly is it that you're maintaining? That such a thing never has been done? Or that such a
thing never can be done? Because there's a difference. If it's the
first, then you're maintaining something you can't prove: you
simply don't have the statistics on every love affair in history.
And even if you did, the undiscovered ones would, by definition,
not be on your list. I grant you that such happinesses may be
rare—as rare even as Stradivarius fiddles; but just as you ought
not to deny the existence of Stradivarii simply because you
haven't come across any, so with the affair in my story.

Lector:　Oh, alright. You needn't go on with the second clunker,
as you call it. I see the point.

Auctor:　Ah! But I am afraid you do not. And in any case, I must
go on because it is your second clunker that will, paradoxically,
lead me to the point of my story. For if you are maintaining that
such a thing as the affair I propose never *can* happen, you have
taken us out of the realm of down-to-earth, historical living—
and even out of the realm of fictional representations of life—
and landed us high in the philosophico-theological sky.

Lector: If that is true, you have no idea how sorry I am for what I have done.

Auctor: Fret not. It is my favorite atmosphere. Pardon me if I change margins and shoulder you off the page for a while.

Lector: But . . .

I'm sure you'll be back. Meanwhile, let me deal at some length with your contention that such happiness *cannot* happen. There are, as I see it, four sets of laws you might invoke to try to justify your position: the *physical,* the *metaphysical,* the *moral,* and the *divine.* I take them up in order.

As to the *physical* impossibility of a long and successful liaison, there simply is none. Physical difficulty, I will grant you: these things are not for the irresolute or the easily spooked. Still, given the necessary robustness of disposition on the part of the lovers concerned, the physical ease of accomplishing their project actually becomes greater as their state of life becomes higher. A house painter in a very small town cannot possibly keep painting the same ladylove's house indefinitely. But a constantly travelling corporate mogul based in a large city has more scope, and thus more opportunity. Presidents have been known to have long affairs indeed. And as for kings . . . well, absolute power enables absolutely, provided only that the parties involved have strong wills, sharp minds, and a modicum of ordinary prudence.

As to the *metaphysical* impossibility of a protracted affair, I deny that as well. There may be philosophical objections to such an arrangement, but there is no a priori necessity for it to fail. The universe is notably indifferent to either good or evil. It leaves ample room for both and does not, despite the prejudices of the more antiquated sort of fiction writers, necessarily punish the lucky, however distasteful you may find their luck.

Moral impossibility, of course, is another matter: there you must make a distinction. If you wish to hold that a love affair in which one of the participants is already married to someone else ought not to be carried on, you are free—and perhaps even well-advised—to do so. But if you wish to maintain that a morally questionable arrangement will by its very nature come a cropper, you are on squishy ground. Hitler was defeated by the Allies, not by his immoral policies—which worked quite long enough and quite well enough to make at least six million Jews despair of a self-enforcing moral law against genocide. Likewise with other cases: those who divorce and remarry do not automatically have wretched lives; and in the matter at hand, adultery is not an inevitable disaster.

Finally, the same reasoning applies to the *divine* law. God is on the record as being flatfootedly opposed to many things, adultery among them. But it has also been told us on high authority indeed that he makes his sun to shine on the just and on the unjust. He has his druthers, therefore; but he does not commonly force them down anyone's throat.

Accordingly, if you encounter—either in the wide world of experience or in the narrower realm of fiction—two people who profess to be quite happy in a questionable arrangement, you may not say to them (or to their creator, in the case of a fiction) that they cannot possibly be happy because there are laws against that sort of thing. You may call them monsters, or fools, or sinners, or anything else that philosophy or theology wants you to call them; but you may not call them liars about their own contentment.

Lector: Excuse me. Do you think it would be possible to interrupt this roll you are on for a question?

Auctor: Not just yet. I have two more items to deal with, so with your permission . . .

. . . I take the liberty of proceeding.

You have called my story unlikely, implying that kings do not fall deeply and permanently in love with parlormaids. I disagree. People fall regularly for all kinds of unlikely types. Senators fall for secretaries, if not pages. CEOs fall for manicurists with nasal voices. Princes fall for showgirls. None of these occurrences is unlikely; most of them are not even rare. The inexorable laws by which you claim they are impossible are in fact regularly overridden by the whimsical but sovereign law of love's gravity. Your problem is that you are confusing *likelihood* and *believability.* That these things happen is simply a fact which, whether it is likely or not, you have no sane choice but to accept. But what you believe about them is a matter of decision on your part. If you are so enamored of your iron laws and dull likelihoods that you do not choose to believe my assertion of the king's and the parlormaid's happiness, you are free once again to do so. But your decision will never be a reason for me to renege on my assertion. I am both less and more enraptured by unlikelihood than you. Less, in that I consider only the totally impossible to be truly unlikely; more, in that I find the allegedly unlikely things in the world far more interesting—and thus more human—than your supposedly likely ones.

You forget what G. K. Chesterton said in *Orthodoxy* on the subject of fairy tales. Imagine one apple tree growing next to another apple tree. You would like to say that it is unlikely that those trees could grow silver candlesticks or golden eggs. But having been taught by Chesterton, I would love to see them do exactly that. I would find the spectacle of silver and gold *objets d'art* sprouting from their branches not one whit less enchanting than I find the apples that more usually grow there. The only thing I would hold to be truly unlikely is that one magical tree plus another magical tree should equal three magical trees; otherwise, I stand ready to welcome anything they might choose to bear, be it nuclear bombs or rubber ducks. For in Elfland—in that adjunct world the human race has wisely built to protect itself from loss of astonishment at this world—the laws of logic apply rigorously but there are no laws of likelihood. Rivers flow with wine to remind us of what should be our constant surprise at the fact that they flow with water. Beasts talk lest we fall prey to chauvinism about our humanity. And all on the premise that it is no more likely that we should talk and dogs should bark than it would be the other way around. It is simply that God in his freedom has done it the way he did— and that, in his freedom, nothing is unlikely: it is simply chosen out of joy.

Which brings me to my second item. The word *happiness* has a fascinating etymology. Its root, *hap-,* appears in such words as *perhaps* and *haply,* but principally in *happen.* In some peculiar way, therefore, happiness has been seen as having something to do with the way things happen—or to give the matter its more usual name, with *luck.* The English language seems to me to be on to something here. Specifically, it is on to the home truth that we cannot, in any ordinary sense, *arrange* for happiness; rather, happiness must somehow *befall* us. This truth is evidenced in many ways, but perhaps the most accessible is the old wisecrack, "The Constitution may guarantee your right to the pursuit of happiness but it doesn't guarantee you'll catch up with it."

I realize that with your love of laws you may find my insistence on happiness as a matter of luck a bit distressing. But think about it. The human race has always—and wisely—been fonder of luck than of law. And for a good reason: what we call laws—at least, what we call physical laws—are not inexorable statutes but simply matters of very high probability. When you get all the way down to the behavior of individual things—of this particular subatomic particle, of that coin being flipped, or of one lonely king in his private chambers—they do pretty much what they please. It is only when you take them by the thousands or billions that something like a law begins to emerge. What emerges, though, never actually becomes a determinative law, only a satisfactorily descriptive one. Counting on the "law" to have its effect, then, is actually more like betting on an almost sure thing: you're practically certain that the apple trees will produce apples; but there's always the remote possibility that they will produce eggs, or tigers hanging by their tails—or nothing at all.

As a race, we have commonly left room for this possibility:

we have called it, variously, a *miracle* or an *act of God*. And lest you think that too theological, remember that your insurance company—whose profits, barring mismanagement, are dependably based on these "laws" of high probability—has been careful to write into your policy a clause indemnifying itself against just such remote possibilities. This actuarial taking of the Lord's name, however, is anything but in vain: even though the actuaries may not spend much time on its theological ramifications, I find its implications significant. Because except for occasional miraculous interventions on God's part, he seems content to run the world very much as a casino owner would run an honest gambling palace. He lets the (unloaded) dice roll the way they want. He lets the cards in the blackjack shoe lie in any (unstacked) order the shuffle determines. He lets the roulette wheel turn at its own (not his) pleasure. And then—precisely and only because he is a master of the odds—he gets the exact result he wants (his profit) *without once interfering with the freedom of anything.*

You may object to this vision of the world as a divine crapshoot, but I think it is as sound as it is factual. We are—*all* things are— free to do whatever we or they choose to have happen. And happiness is simply our word for *a felicitous tissue of such happenings*— just as unhappiness is our name for a dire one. Or to put the matter more carefully, happiness lies in our ability to accept everything that happens and then either enjoy it gratefully or reconcile it patiently. We may not be able to control all of the things that happen outside us, or even very many of the things that happen inside us; but since we are in control of both our gratitude and our patience, there is always and in every circumstance a path open to the happiness that God already has over everything. Such happiness is not cheap, of course: it cost even God some terrible hours on the cross. But it is available—and my story, despite its shortcomings and triviality, was designed to display just that availability.

For the king and the parlormaid are both paradigms of the

gratitude and patience that brings happiness out of mere happening. The king, alone by his fire, in no way willed beforehand his infatuation with the girl; the girl, bringing him his dinner for the hundredth time, had not decided that tonight was the night to declare her silent love. It was the mix-up in the kitchen that broke the ice. The two of them contributed only the good-humored gratitude that enabled them to enjoy the meal and evening at the beginning of the story, and the stouthearted patience with their affair's details that earned them the superimposed accolade at its end. They took a gift gracefully; I will not allow your preoccupation with law and likelihood to take the edge off their triumph. And now, at long last . . .

. . . I will let you back in from the margin.

Lector: Thank you, I think. Let me say first that while you have earned a few points on my card as to your intentions in telling the story, I am by no means disposed to take back all of my objections to it. I am willing, however, to let them pass for the moment if you will hear me out on some proposals I have for you.

Auctor: Fair enough. Propose away.

Lector: I realize you have your reasons for wanting the broad outlines of your story to stand as written. But don't you think that some of its—I do not mean to worry the bone of my contention, but the word seems just—some of its *offensiveness* could be mitigated by altering a few details?

Auctor: I am reasonable: anything I can do to please you, I will. On the other hand, I am not cheap: I cannot poke in changes that give away my story just to make the odd buck of palatability. State the alterations you have in mind. I shall see what I can do.

Lector: Well, my first suggestion is that you make the king a bachelor at the beginning of the story, thus removing the (as I see them) presently gratuitous stigmas of injustice and infidelity with which you have burdened him.

Auctor: Hmm. I see. Perhaps it would be better if you made all your suggestions at once. That way, I can avoid repetition in my replies.

Lector: Very well. My second idea, should you not like the first, is that you arrange for the queen's death, thus freeing the king to pursue a legitimate relationship with his love. Authors do such things all the time. If a character in a TV series can be run over by a truck for no better reason than that the actress playing the part wants to do a movie, surely you can dispose of the lady in question for the sake of moral probity.

My third proposal is more radical: leave the queen in the script; let the king and the parlormaid realize and declare their mutual love; even give them—if you must—their night of passion; but then have them come to their senses, do the upright thing, and make a grand renunciation of each other. MUSIC UP and all that sort of thing as the girl goes gracefully into a convent. Abelard and Heloise all over again.

If none of those pleases you, however, you could always have the king, or the parlormaid, or both of them, die not too long after they embark on their affair. That would give you time to make your point about happiness—it would even serve as a kind of "ever after"—but it would not so ham-fistedly go against the grain of moral sensitivity as does your present version. There. That's about it. What do you think?

Auctor: Dear me! I'm afraid I think less of each successive proposal and least of all of the last. Still . . .

. . . let me give you my reasons as briefly as I can.

As to your first suggestion—about making the king a bachelor—it simply will not work. You seem to imagine that by making him marriageable, you can legitimize the affair. But you forget a lesson of history. If Edward VIII—the world's most eligible bachelor in his day—could not marry Wallis Simpson because she was a commoner, my king could certainly not marry a parlormaid who was not only a commoner but lower-class to boot. You may argue of course that he could, like the noble Edward, renounce his throne for the woman he loved; but to me, that will not wash. Half a lifetime living exiled in the delta of a great fortune with nothing much to do is not my recipe for living happily ever after. Retirement is bad enough; early retirement is a snare and a delusion. I am sorry, but I simply will not have it.

Your second idea is even more unacceptable. Not only does putting out a contract on the queen leave you with the Edward VIII quandary still in effect; worse still, it involves you in a contradiction of the very principle in whose name you propose the fell deed. You urge me to get on with the job because "authors do such things all the time"; and you say that it is "for the sake of moral probity" that you want me to do the poor woman in. But in fact only desperate and shabby authors ever do such things; and while they may do them for the sake of any number of disreputable ends—like keeping their jobs or getting rid of characters they have lost their way with—they cannot with a straight face do them in the name of moral principle. Think, please, what you are asking me to do! To avoid adultery, you want me to resort to murder. Not only that, but you seem to have a lofty and unwriterly notion of what an author must do to get rid of a character. The details have to be worked out; no mere wave of the hand will do the trick. For example: will the queen depart this vale of tears quickly or slowly? If quickly, will it be by prussic acid in her almond blancmange, by an embolism in her brain, or by structural collapse of the tower in which she is saying her prayers? If slowly, will it be the work of bone cancer, tuberculosis, or undiagnosed syphilis? But perhaps you see: however I might contrive the outcome you want, I myself, for the time of contriving it, would be nothing more than a hit man. You may think the woman's life of teas, country fairs, and domestic squabbling despicable. But she is a human being nonetheless, and I will not have blood on my hands just to shield chaste eyes from royal peccadilloes.

Your last two proposals have, between them, all the drawbacks of the first two, plus the added burden of silliness. The grand renunciation you suggest would be no favor to my happy couple; it would be just a sop thrown to minds already soppy enough. Abelard and Heloise indeed! That they found some other happiness than the one they first discovered, I will not deny. But it came at the price of denying the metaphysical possibility of their first happiness; and so, for all the reasons I have already given you, I will neither castrate my king nor immure my parlormaid just to trick them out with some other form of bliss, however profound. And as for littering the stage with corpses—of lover, or beloved, or both—come now! This is not a rerun of "Miami Vice," it is a love story. If you force me to choose between sex and violence, I will choose sex every time. I may be out of step with much of history and all of the present age, but that's the way I am: "Love, not War," is my motto. Sorry, then—but a resounding no to all your suggestions.

Lector: Well, I tried. I only hope that now, having exhausted the matter of your story, we may get on with the subjects of health, money, and love.

Auctor: Unfortunately, far from having exhausted the matter, we have just arrived at the heart of it.

Lector: I was afraid of something like that. What then, may I ask, is next?

Auctor: Next I shall take up your real problem, which is that you are not actually interested in happiness at all. Every time the subject comes up, you promptly substitute another subject for it.

Lector: And you will, naturally, tell me what that other subject is?

Auctor: Naturally. It is *religion.* Turn the page and I shall tell you what I mean.

3

Interlude

MY AGENDA FOR THIS CHAPTER HAS THREE ITEMS ON IT. FIRST, I'm going to tell you something about what religion is; second, I want to tell you about something—namely, Christianity—that isn't religion; and third, I'm going to prove to you that even though no religion can possibly deliver what it promises, we go right on buying model after model in the hope that it will. Admittedly, my use of the word *religion* may strike you as odd at first—and my insistence that religion is the major roadblock to your own pursuit of happiness may irk you mightily. Bear with me: in the end, I think you will find me merely accurate.

Item One: A Definition of Religion

When we talk about *religion,* we use the word in two different senses. The first is wide and loose: we say, for example, that Arthur jogs *religiously,* meaning that he is devoted to his daily regimen of running. Or we speak of *the religious life,* referring either to what goes on in convents and monasteries, or to the practice of prayer and good works by less formally committed citizens. Or we distinguish between organized and unorganized *religion,* usually implying that the unorganized variety is somehow more sincere and praiseworthy. But in all of these usages we are not so much talking about the nature of religion itself as we are about the virtues or vices of the persons practicing a particular religion. Arthur's "religious" padding along the roads may be seen by us as either a healthy commitment or an insane monomania. A nun entering the "religious" life may be thought of as either running toward or running away from reality. Those who devote themselves to Episcopalianism, Reformed Judaism, Methodism, Islam, or even some home-brewed concoction of Oriental philosophy and California cuisine, can be judged as foolish, fanatical, or just fine. But in every case, it is chiefly *religionists*—not religion—that these loose usages pay attention to.

My only purpose in mentioning this wide and floppy sense of religion is to get it off the table. I am not concerned here with value judgments about the individual religiosities of our neighbors; I want to be as precise as possible about religion itself. Accordingly, to get us going in the direction of the narrower and more strict sense of the word, here is a working definition.

Religion is the attempt on the part of human beings to establish a right relationship between themselves and something outside themselves— something they think to be of life-shaping importance. Notice that I have deliberately left most of the details out of this definition. The nature of the *attempt* is yet to be specified: it could involve thoughts, words, or deeds, and it could entail anything from meditating on a mantra to feeding your firstborn to crocodiles. Likewise, the *right relationship* is still undefined: it might be one of harmony and union, or of cautiousness and control, or even of fear and total avoidance. Finally, the *something outside themselves* is very much up for grabs: it could be God, or the goddess, or the gods, or Satan; but it could also be nature, happiness, fate, the forces of the universe, the spirits of the dead—or, to my point in this book, health, money, or love.

In any case, on this definition, religion is an attempt to influence someone or something; and it invariably results in the creation of a program designed to exert such influence. This program may be about God, or the good life, or good sex. It may be strenuous or relaxed. It may call for the commitment of a lifetime or need only the whim of a moment. But whatever its incidental variations of goal or style, it will always have three essential characteristics: it will involve a *creed;* it will demand specific *cultic* practices; and it will insist on certain patterns of *conduct* in its adherents. Creed, Cult, and Conduct, then—the three Cs of the program of religion. Let me flesh them out briefly.

Creed encompasses everything we *think* (or *believe,* to use the word loosely) when we undertake the program of a particular religion. Such thoughts may involve subjects as diverse as God, money, Satan, or jogging for your health. They may amount to nothing more than vague attitudes of approval or disapproval, or they may entail subscription to an entire body of formal doctrine. "The universe is nice," for example, is a possible creed—as is, "God couldn't possibly care whether I eat meat on Fridays or not." But so too is the whole of the Westminster Catechism, or the Augsburg Confession, or the Creed of Pius V, or the Qur'an, or the Book of Mormon, or any other body of doctrine about anything—up to and including the collected works of Adele Davis or L. Ron Hubbard. In every case, though, each such creed will turn out to be a formula for thinking about the "something outside ourselves"—an intellectual recipe which, *if you get it right,* promises to give you the influence you want over the something you have in mind.

Cult stands for all the *liturgical practices* our religion's program calls for. These can range from chicken sacrifices at dawn, to Morning Prayer and Sermon on Sundays, to not eating saturated fats, to transcendental meditation, to owning a house in the Hamptons. At first glance, this spectrum of practices may look like nothing more than individual preference at work; but in fact, the particular "liturgies" we engage in are almost always dictated socially, by our coreligionists—by our fellow Episcopalians, possibly, or by our fellow health nuts, or by our fellow yuppies. Our *creed* may be a private matter, but our *cultic practices* are always public: even when I am driving alone in my Mercedes, I am being driven by the liturgical requirements of the church of the upwardly mobile. In the last analysis, therefore, all such practices, conventionally pious or not, are undertaken precisely for *religious* reasons: we do them on the assumption (once again) that *if we get them right,* the relationship we are seeking to establish (not only with the "something outside" but with the community of our fellow seekers) will become a reality.

Conduct, finally, covers the rest of the territory of religion: it stands generally for the behavioral requirements that the program of our religion lays upon us, but specifically for the *moral* aspects of those requirements. Please note, though, that I don't have in mind any specific system of morality. Depending on the particulars of our program, we could earn a religious good conduct medal by having one wife, or two wives, or none—or simply by never marrying our mother-in-law. We could give all our goods to the poor or we could keep them for ourselves. We could do justice or exterminate whole races. We could liberate the oppressed or call for the assassination of authors we didn't like. Or—to run out the list at random—we could lift weights, eat yogurt, wear garlic around our necks, or not step on sidewalk cracks. But once again, and for the last time: every one of these things—when done as part of the program of a religion—would be done on the assumption that *if we got it right,* it would land us in the New Jerusalem, or the Old Eden, or the Good Life—or whatever state our religion names as the fulfillment of the relationship we desire.

Now then. I want you to note two things about religion as I have so far defined it. The first is that it always insists on *our getting the entire business right.* To be sure, there are kindly religions in which God or the gods promise to help you get it right; and there are religions so relaxed that there is almost nothing you can get wrong.

But in every religion there is always something that simply must be gotten right; and so in the long run, the relationship desired is ultimately *up to us.* If we fail, we're out of luck: the "something outside ourselves" can have only one word to say to us: "Sorry, Charlie; no relationship." And therefore, since we always fail somewhere, our attitude toward the all-important something turns out to be anything but fondness and warm toasties; rather, it becomes one of apprehension, if not downright fear—a state of perpetual jitters at being charged with malpractice over some item of creed, cult, or conduct. Religion commonly professes to love the something it's trying to establish a relationship with; but in fact its program is aimed less at love than at such things as appeasement, propitiation, self-protection, conjuring, and control.

And as if that weren't bad enough, there is a second thing to be noted: none of the religious "business" we try so hard to get right—none of the stipulated religious perfections, creedal, cultic, or behavioral—has any *necessary or dependably effective* connection with the relationship sought. None of it *works.* You can pour out your son's blood as a sacrifice on the stones of the piazza and you can bury his body in the foundation of the city walls; but a big enough army can take your town anyway. You can conform intellectually to every scrap of your creed and still be hit on the head by a loose gargoyle off a buttress of the cathedral. You can fast three days a week and eat nothing but broccoli and brown rice the other four and still die of pneumonia, if not malnutrition. And you can be as good as gold—but if the powers that be decide they don't like the cut of your jib, you can also spend the rest of a long life in prison, or of a short one at the end of a rope.

But for the third and finally devastating thing, nobody ever succeeds in achieving all the stipulated perfections anyway. By a combination of Murphy's Law and catch-22, religion regularly backfires on its adherents. You piously shed your son's blood, but by accident you pour it on the wrong part of the piazza: the gods look away, the enemy marches in—and you go directly to religious jail. You believe all the right things only to be told that the old revelation was wrong: after twenty years on brown rice, you find out you were supposed to have been eating bulgur wheat instead. But above all, you never quite succeed at being as good as gold. The museum of perfect people—in which your religion promised you enshrinement—turns out to be empty. Nobody ever got a hundred on the tests that religion imposes; but since a hundred is the only score religion is interested in, religion is finally interested in nobody.

The net result of it all is just one thing: besides being ineffective and impossible to fulfil, *religion is no fun.* It may begin by holding out the carrot of approval; but it always ends up beating us with the stick of condemnation. It is a mirthless subject which, if we thought about it carefully for two minutes, no sane (and certainly no fun-loving) person would have any truck with. And yet it remains the human race's favorite subject—the one to which, millennium after millennium and at all hours of the day and night, we constantly . . . But put that thought on hold for a bit while I turn to

Item Two: Christianity As No Religion

In spite of the fact that the Good News of Jesus Christ (to give Christianity one of its own titles of preference) has been seen as a religion by outsiders and been sold as one by its adherents, it is not a religion at all. Rather, it is the announcement of *the end of religion.* On its plain, New Testament face, it proclaims that all the things that religion promised but couldn't deliver have been delivered once and for all by Jesus in his death and resurrection. This is not to say that there isn't plenty of old-time religion in the Bible; there are in fact enough creedal, cultic, and behavioral stipulations to gladden the heart of an Aztec priest. And those requirements can be found not only in the Old Testament (where they are obviously meant to be taken seriously) but also in the New (where they cannot be taken with anything like the seriousness they are often accorded).

Nevertheless, on any final, Gospel-regarding balance, only one conclusion is possible: religion as I have defined it—that is, religion as something that human beings must get right in order to have a correct relationship with God—is a subject that shouldn't be given Christian houseroom.

It has been argued, of course, that this "no-religion" aspect of the Gospel—this insistence on salvation by grace alone, not works (not even religious works)—is the invention of Paul rather than Jesus. You yourself may even have bought that bill of goods. For me, though, it just won't wash.

In the first place, its fundamental proposition—namely, that the "simple Jesus of the Gospels" was surreptitiously replaced by the "complex Christ of Paul"—runs clean contrary to the evidence of history. The records simply do not support the nineteenth-century fantasy that a cosmic savior who reconciles all by grace through faith was somehow slipped over on a primitive church that previously had heard only of a wonder-working rabbi with a few religious improvements up his sleeve. The early church was reading Paul's letters before he died in A.D. 64; it did not, however, get its hands on the Gospels as we now have them until sometime after that (65, say, to 110). The Gospels, accordingly, were written for the sake of the Epistles, not the other way around. At the very least, the two were accepted by the church in a process of mutual interaction: there was never even a hint that the first Christians thought one of them was seditiously infiltrating the other.

Paradoxically, moreover, the four Gospels the church finally settled on as "canonical" (Matthew, Mark, Luke, and John—their predominance is clearly evident by 150 to 200) were the four so-called "simpler" ones as contrasted with the other, more high-flown examples of the genre now generally referred to as the Apocryphal Gospels. It would seem, therefore, that however much the 19th (and 20th) centuries may have found this "simple-complex" combination indigestible, the early church, if it noticed it at all, took it in as nothing more than two courses in the same delicious meal.

In the second place, the New Testament has a perfectly good answer to the charge that Christianity as we now have it is radically Pauline. And the answer is that God hired Paul (then called Saul) on the road to Damascus for the precise purpose of making Christianity Pauline—that is, of rescuing it from the overly "religious" orientation of the exclusively Jewish-Christian Jerusalem church. The main item in Paul's job description was precisely that he knock religion in the head. Because whatever it was that Jesus may have thought or taught (and at the very least, the authorities who finally nailed him didn't think he was teaching *their* brand of religion), it soon became evident that if the original Jerusalem church crowd could have had their way, Christianity would have been swamped in a flood of religious requirements like circumcision, dietary laws, and other gentile-excluding practices. Indeed, in an odd moment, I once suggested that what Jesus actually said to Saul on the Damascus road was not, "Saul, Saul, why do you persecute me?" but, "Saul! Help! I'm a prisoner in a commandment factory."

In other words, far from supplanting the Gospel of Jesus Christ, Paul actually rescued the Good News of Jesus from the danger of being converted into the bad news of religion. He was the one who saw clearly that if Jesus had indeed done whatever it was that religion had been trying to do, there was simply no more need for religion. Its job (which it couldn't really accomplish anyway) had been done for it. The whole business was over. All that we or anyone had to do now was *believe* (have *faith*) in Jesus and we would be home free because the right relationship, so long and so vainly sought, was already a fact in him. There were no works of any kind we had to get right to achieve the relationship; we had only to *trust* him and be pleasantly surprised at the light burden he had substituted for the iron yoke of religion.

Admittedly—and legitimately—Christianity has long made use of the *forms* of religion in presenting its radically nonreligious message. It has employed the trappings of creed, cult, and conduct freely and without apology. But it has never used them seriously: at its Gospel-regarding best, it has always said that those trappings had no *religious* function. Christians used them not to do the job of establishing a right relationship with God but simply to remind themselves of what the job was that needed doing—and of the rib-tickling fact that Jesus had done the whole thing free for nothing. When we get right down to it, therefore, there is not a single properly religious act in the Christian "religion." Our confessions do not earn us forgiveness by their sincerity or their exhaustiveness: we had it all along by Jesus' gift. Our prayers do not con God into being gracious: he conned himself on the cross. Our Eucharists do not cause Jesus to show up in a place from which he was absent: he is already everywhere—in all the fullness of his reconciling work—before the service starts. And our baptisms (to come finally to the root sacrament of the Good News) do not divide the world into the saved (us, inside) and the lost (them, outside). Baptism—and the church it constitutes—is simply the authentic, effective sign of the *mystery of the Christ* who has already saved all, whether in or out. Accordingly, none of these "religious" acts leaves room for a single, saving thing that is *up to us*. We erect the sacramental signs, yes; but the mystery beneath the signs is none of our doing. We have only to believe that we have all been *drawn in for good by Jesus* ("I, if I be lifted up from the earth, will draw *all* to myself," John 12:32) and laugh out loud.

That is why the Gospel alone is Good News and all the religions of the world—whether they're about God or some lesser thing—are bad news. You would think, therefore, wouldn't you, that the world would take one look at the "Gone Out Of The Religion Business" sign on the door of the church and come pouring in to celebrate the free gift. Well, if you did, you would think wrong. Because not only doesn't the world knock down the church's door; it actually prefers to sit outside in the cold wind of religion and make believe it's earning its way home by shivering. Worse yet, the church—at most times and in all ages—has either not bothered to put the sign up, or has been feverishly busy taking it down. All of which is a sad, silly story that we can pursue at leisure later on in this book. Right now, we have had just enough of it to bring me to *Item three* on my agenda:

Religion As Everybody's Favorite Subject, Bar None

We have arrived back at my charge against you at the end of our dialogue about the king and the parlormaid. As you no doubt see now, the precise fault I found in your suggested improvements to my story was your compulsion to substitute religious programs for the bare-bottomed but successful pursuit of happiness I allowed my fictive couple. You tried to get me to foist upon them every one of the three Cs.

Take *creed,* for example: you were itching to have them subscribe to an unrealistically tit-for-tat view of the universe in which naughty people invariably suffer for their naughtiness. Or take *cult:* you tried to stipulate expensive sacrifices just to avoid the embarrassment of free happiness; visions of dead queens, kings, and parlormaids gave you no rest until some bloodthirsty ritual of expiation could reassure you that the price of happiness had been paid. Or finally, take *conduct:* you insisted that they undertake some stagey course of reform before you would allow them any "real" happiness at all; haunted by noble speeches of renunciation and the sound of convent doors banging shut, you were not in the least disturbed by the fact that your several suggested courses for their pursuit of happiness would probably have led to nothing but misery.

To all of that "religious programming" I have only two things to say. First, none of it could have *necessitated* anything, whether in fiction or in real life: if they ended up contented at the end of your prescribed religious exercises, it would not have been a consequence of their pursuing the exercises but simply the result of their having, by grace and forgiveness, accepted the luck of whatever draw they made. Religion, as a device for insuring anything, *just doesn't work.* Second, though—and much more important—if the Gospel is indeed the end of religion, then the Gospel itself would not enjoin upon them even the smallest smitch of your religious program of improvement. It would have assured them of their reconciliation in the mystery of Jesus' new creation, and invited them to *believe him.* What they did after that might be wise or foolish, just or unjust; but *none of it would have been a condition* without which Jesus' reconciliation of them would have been void. Once again, I realize that this is not the usual way the Gospel is marketed; but it is the original factory specification and I have no intention of apologizing for it.

Still, let me meet you halfway. While religion remains a subject that has nothing to do with the price of happiness, I still owe you a demonstration of how all of us go blithely on assuming, in every department of our lives, that it does.

Think, therefore, of life as a school—as a kindergarten filled mostly with fun and games, if you like, or as an austere college of hard knocks. Whichever way you imagine it, there will always be courses, from Sandbox to Suffering, that we cannot avoid taking. *Health, Money,* and *Love* are three such offerings—major subjects, if you will; but so are courses like *Growing Up, Running a Family, Relating To One's Parents, Working For A Living, Enjoying One's Leisure, Being Sick, Getting Old,* and finally, *Dying.* But these major subjects are always tough courses. *Dying 101,* for example, is never easy. The *Family Life* sequence may start out as a lark, but somewhere around *Teenage Children 201,* or *Seven-Year Itch 303,* failure seems unavoidable. And so instead of facing the rigors of the subjects themselves, we regularly substitute a minor we think we can pass— and that minor is invariably religion.

For instance. Instead of dealing with death, we conjure with assorted religions that we think will enable us to avoid it. We may pursue the tyrannical cult of youth, hoping against hope that if we remain flat of tum and firm of bum, death will never darken our door. Or we may try, by good behavior, to bargain God out of his obvious insistence on the subject. Or we may work up a creedal structure in which the tiger of death is turned into a metaphysical pussycat. And even though none of these programs of study in the least excuses us from having to take the main course from start to finish, we go right on giving all of our time and attention to the substitute minor.

Another instance. It is one of the hard facts of life that there is no necessary correspondence between the work you do and the rewards others give you for doing it. I can be paid $3,000 for a magazine piece that takes me a week to complete, or $3,000 for a book that consumes a year of my life. You may earn $300,000 for eight phone calls and a consultation, or nothing at all for six months' worth of patient design work that gets lost in the shuffle of office politics. Yet instead of looking at the satisfaction of work well done, both you and I persist in giving our chief attention to the religion of money—a religion which, as you well know, holds that we are no good at all unless we are paid in exact proportion to our efforts—or beyond all proportion, whichever shall first occur. Alternatively, we may decide that since the whole business of business is a fraud, we will cook up for ourselves a religion of winning the lottery by playing the birth dates of our children— thus offering up the kiddies' food money as a whole burnt offering to the mindless god of beating the system.

But perhaps you see the point: whether the major subject is Health, Money, Love, or anything else, our religions become substitutes that do nothing but cut us off from whatever happiness we might, by gratitude or forgiveness, have gotten while taking the courses.

I have a feeling, though, that you still remain uneasy. You have a gnawing sense that I have given you a fast shuffle: my definition of religion has, you think, reduced it to little more than superstition. I propose, therefore, to end this chapter by conceding as many of your objections as I can, and then coming full circle and claiming that even at that, my definition still holds. Here goes.

Yes, religion can be seen as having its merits. And yes, I have left them out of account. So to set the record straight, here are a few of them. For one thing, religion has been the human race's constant witness to the fact that we are *not* in the rightest of relationships, either with something outside ourselves, or with our neighbors, or even with ourselves. For another, it has borne testimony to the fact that something needs to be done about our chronic failing of life's major courses: we are too often *not* good parents, good husbands, good lovers, good livers, or good diers—and religion has never ceased to be a nagging reminder of those deficiencies. But by the very nature of religion, none of that nagging has ever succeeded in eliminating even a single one of them from the world. To paraphrase the author of the Epistle to the Hebrews, "It is impossible that the blood of bulls and goats can take away deficiencies of our own devising." And as we might add, it is equally impossible that any kind of religion can alter the luck of the draw by which God is content to have life provide us with deficiencies *not* of our own devising. So it hardly matters if I equate religion and superstition. The difference between them lies solely in the assumed respectability of the devices and programs they use. Religion may enjoin upon you weighty and important things like not lying or having only one husband; superstition, by contrast, may give you silly things like not getting on a plane unless you have hung up the bath towel with the label out of sight. But in no case is there any difference between them when it comes to their respective abilities to deliver the improvements they promise. Telling the truth can get you in royal dutch. Staying married to the same man can give you ulcers. And you can hide all the towel labels in the world and still not stop a terrorist's bomb from going off at 30,000 feet. One last time: *none of it necessarily works*.

But now I hear a subsidiary objection forming in your mind. You want to suggest to me that maybe a "good" religion—a God-endorsed, God-revealed religion—might work if God had promised to respond to our religious acts with suitably direct and miraculous action of his own. Well, of course it might. But you've got a big "if" in there. Because when you actually look at the Christian version of the revelation of God, it becomes clear that he has promised no such thing. True enough, he has at times and places intervened with miracles—but largely on his own motion, and certainly not as a quid pro quo for correct religious behavior. The notion that we are to be in a constant state of "praying for miracles" is dead wrong. The common New Testament word for "miracle" is the ordinary Greek word for "sign"; and nobody is smart enough to know in advance what sign to pray for, or even to recognize the sign correctly when it comes up. If it's getting dark, for example, and your gas is running low and you have to get to your aunt's house in fifteen minutes or less, what sign do you want to see? Auntie's House, 1 Mi., that's what. But is that the sign you need? Suppose the sign you actually get says, Bridge Out, 1,000 Ft. What do you do? Step on the gas and try to make it anyway because you didn't get your miracle? Or stop dead and turn around because you did? See what I mean?

Besides, if you put all the miracles ever wrought into one pile, they would look like a grain of sand compared to the galaxies-ful of noninterventionist, luck-of-the-draw operations by which God normally lets the world run itself. And do you see what *that* means? People always talk as if miracles were the holy things and ordinary events were simply profane. But if God's all-but-total way of managing the universe is simply chance (which, even in the Bible, it certainly is—biblical grass grew mostly by luck or by gorry, and biblical rain fell the same way), then luck is just as holy as miracle because it's just as much God's way of doing business. Maybe it's even holier, because he seems to like working by it a lot more of the time. And you don't even have to single out *good* luck for the accolade: as Charles Williams was fond of saying, "*All* luck is holy"—for the simple reason that all luck, good or bad, is God's chosen métier.

That, then, is what's really wrong with religion even after you've given it all the good marks you can: it rejects God's holy luck and tries to substitute for it our own sticky-fingered control. That it does so on the pretense of guaranteeing our happiness is not only irrelevant but wrong. *Happiness* (to say it once again) is from *happen,* and what happens is almost entirely *luck*—good, bad, or indifferent. And therefore nobody whose chief business is trying to find some way of jimmying the happenings of the world into a religious line can ever possibly be happy—for the simple reason that he is forsaking the acceptance of God's reality for the illusion of his own control.

And there, too, is the reason I told you my story of the king and the parlormaid as I did. It was to confront you with raw, scandalous luck—and with all the religious contortions that were your immediate response to it. But it was also to lead you to a respect for the holiness of luck—of mere happening—without which no happiness is possible. Now, however, we have to go much deeper: let me tell you another story . . .

4

Story

═════════

1 *Once before all time, there was a Lover, a Beloved, and a magical Bed in which they played out the unity of their love.* *²The joy of the two of them in that Bed was complete: there was nothing besides their love, and there was nothing they needed to make their happiness more perfect.*

3 But one endless afternoon as they rested in the Bed after long love, the Lover laid his head next to the Beloved's and began to whisper a story in her ear. *⁴He told her of strange and wonderful happenings; he spoke of a day when the nothing besides their love would teem with things.* *⁵He told her tales of the things themselves: of the fiery outburst that would be the beginning of them; of the blazing dance that would be the continuance of them;* *⁶of the gorgeous singularities that would be the flowering of them; and of the endless delight that would be the fulfillment of them.*

7 And as he spoke in that Bed, his Beloved whispered back to him the name of each of the things in his story, calling them all out of nothing into being by her words. 8She said "stars" and suddenly the Bed was full of stars; she said "planets" and planets whirled around their heads. 9She said "water" and floods washed over them; she said "wheat" and there was wheat; she said "grapes" and there were catawba, and scuppernong, and cabernet sauvignon. 10She said "fish" and "birds" and "beasts"—she called forth porgies and sharks, hummingbirds and vultures, mice and mammoths—and they sported before them in all their kinds and numbers.

11 Then she said, "Monique," and "Arthur," and "Harry," and "Martha," and there were children and women and men everywhere dancing their way home to them in the Bed. 12And even though the things she spoke into being danced in their own seasons and to their own measures—even though to themselves they seemed to come and go—they and their dancing were continually held in being by her voice.

13 And she gathered them all together into a single diamond no bigger than a peppercorn and placed it in her Lover's palm to hold forever. 14And the diamond was beautiful, and its beauty could never be lost. For if any part of it, in any of its seasons or measures, made itself ugly, she immediately spoke its true name and restored its true beauty. 15And the Lover saw the diamond, and he loved it, and he loved the Beloved because of it. 16And they and the diamond rested in their mutual Bed; and they all lived happily ever after.

Now then. That may strike you as a longish fetch from the first chapter of the Book of Genesis, and an even longer one from the subjects of health, money, and love. But it isn't. And if you can muster up a little patience with me, I'll show you why.

THE STORY, EXPOUNDED

Verse 1: on the matter of *gender.*

In spite of what you may think, there is nothing coy about my story
and there will be nothing coy in my exposition of it. This verse,
quite simply, is about the Holy and Undivided Trinity—about
God as Christians worship him. I will admit that my image of lovers
in bed is not the commonest device used to expound the doctrine
of the Trinity, and I grant you that it may sound a bit trendy, with
its overtones of the sexual revolution and the equal rights movement. But in fact, the image is commoner than you think, and my
use of it is anything but up-to-date.

The basic device goes all the way back to St. Augustine, who
held that the Father, the Son, and the Holy Spirit could quite
properly be viewed as *Amans, Amatus,* and *Amor Mutuus:* that is, as
the divine *Lover,* the divine *Beloved,* and the divine *Mutual Love.* No
doubt, of course, he did not imagine the Beloved as feminine; in
all likelihood, he was simply picking up on the Father's words to
Jesus at his baptism: "This is my beloved Son." But Augustine also
knew two important things. The first was that in some profound
way God in himself is totally beyond all distinctions of gender; the
second, however, was that Scripture nevertheless freely uses all three
genders when speaking of God.

Consider. Quite plainly, the first Person of the Trinity—the
Father—is masculine. In my narration, accordingly, I have remained utterly traditional as to his gender: he is the Lover, the
divine Boyfriend.

But when you come to the second Person, the eternal *Son,*
the divine *Word* who becomes incarnate in the *Lord* Jesus, Scripture
gives you a choice. Commonly, of course, that eternal Word is
masculine: in both Hebrew and Greek, *Son, Word,* and *Lord* are all
masculine nouns. But this second Person, this eternal Word who
is the actual agent of creation—the one who, by speaking the name
of each thing the Father thinks up, brings all things out of nothing

into being—is also referred to in another gender. She is the holy *Wisdom,* a title which, in Hebrew, Greek, and Latin, is feminine.

You never heard of such a thing? Ah, but perhaps you have. The Church of the Holy Wisdom in Constantinople (once a Christian edifice dedicated to Jesus as the incarnate Wisdom of God, but now a mosque in modern Istanbul) was called *Hagia Sophia* in Greek and *Sancta Sophia* in Latin—both of which work out in English to *Saint Sophie.* So Jesus, besides having called himself a mother hen, has also been called by a woman's name for a very long time by a large number of his most orthodox followers. All of which seems to me quite sufficient warrant for my depicting the second Person of the Trinity as the divine Lover's Girlfriend.

The argument, therefore, that I ought not to do such a thing because it violates tradition falls flat on its face. But there is another argument against this kind of larking around with gender in the case of God, and it needs answering before we go on. You hear people prattling on nowadays about the notion that our language about God should be "non-gender-specific"—that we should go miles out of our way not only to avoid calling God "he," "she," or "it," but that we should also eschew all titles (such as "Father," "Lord," or "Mother") that in any way specify gender. Frankly, I find the whole notion silly and inconvenient, but here's a reasoned answer to it anyway.

The supposed grounds for refusing to predicate gender of God is that God, as God, is beyond gender. Well, of course he (or she, or it) is. But if you're going to insist on talking that way, you are obliged to say that God is beyond *any* category of ours. (Even if you say something as minimal as "God *is,*" for example, you are in over your head: God's is-ness and ours are in two different leagues.) But since we have no experience of anything except our own categories—and especially since we have nevertheless felt free to use those categories *analogically,* even when we knew they didn't apply directly—it's positively inhuman to deprive ourselves of them. Because all that does is make our talk about God dull. So as far as I'm concerned, when we imagine God as masculine, or feminine, or neuter, we neither insult him nor do we capitulate to linguistic chauvinism. We simply take three things we are already captivated by and apply them to the God who we believe is preeminently captivating—to the her (or the it, or the him) who is the *Mysterium Tremendum et Fascinans.* So I have no apologies. Not for making God the Father a Boyfriend; not for making God the Son a Girlfriend; and not for making God the Holy Spirit (*spirit,* in Greek at least, is neuter) a Mattress and Box Spring. To me, the more gender we can get into the act, the better. That's already the way it works out here, and for my money that makes it the best clue to the way we ought to imagine it working out hereafter.

Verse 2: the Holy Spirit as a *magical Bed.*

Most of the images we form of God in the act of making the world are derived from the crafts or the arts. Take God as the Infinite Watchmaker, for example: the picture you get is one of an omnipotent, omniscient Swiss craftsman, patiently assembling the universe with a jeweler's loupe stuck in his left eye. Or take God as the Infinite Novelist: what is conjured up by that is the image of a creative genius who brings forth not just fictions but realities— solid places, tangible things, panting people—whom he leaves free to play out their several characters in the dance of their interactions. This second image is a lot better than the first; but neither is as good as the image of God as Magician. Because only magic captures the ease with which God creates, the total lack of necessity by which he operates, and the vast exuberance with which he tosses off his effects. The world is not the grimy result of divine sweat, nor is it the inevitable result of the divine nature, nor is it the unenviable result of divine loneliness. It is the crazy result of the divine *Abracadabra!*

Think about that. Just as a magician is free to produce either a rabbit or a lark from the hat—and equally free to produce either of them by saying *Abracadabra!* or by saying *Shazzam!*—so God is free to produce whatever he (or they, or she, or it) wants by saying whatever he wants. That there should be a rabbit as a result of the divine pronouncement of *Rabbit!* is neither more nor less remarkable than that there should be Alpha Centauri as a result of the divine *Alpha Centauri!* We love magic precisely because there is no necessity about the words spoken, and no proportion between them and their results. And we love the absence of necessity and the presence of disproportion because they lie at the very root of our being—because we come from a magical Home, from a happy Bed in which everything is done for a lark. Watchmaking is work, and novel writing is slow going; but magic is fun, and we love it because we ourselves come out of the divine Fun in Bed.

Verses 3-6: the word *happenings.*

We have talked before about the connection between *happen, happiness,* and *luck.* All I want to emphasize here is that that connection, too, lies at the root of our being. For creation is nothing less than what God *lets happen.* In the Hebrew original of the Book of Genesis, and in the Greek and Latin versions, God's creating words are all in the imperative: they sound like carefully thought out commands issued as the result of a divine plan. But in English at least (because we lack a one-word form for the third person imperative), there is a nice freedom about them. He says, "*Let there be* light" . . . or "a firmament in the midst of the waters" . . . or "swarms of living creatures." He (or she, or it, or they; I promise you: this is the last time I shall run up the warning flag of gender or number over the three Persons who are the one God)—they even say, at the end, "*Let us make man in our own image.* . . ."

Do you see? God *lets* everything be, himself included. He creates the world out of his divine freedom and he lets it continue in its own freedom. And therefore the image of the creative act now changes. God is neither Watchmaker, nor Novelist, nor even Magician; he is the Divine Child in the bathtub, blowing bubbles through the circle of his thumb and forefinger. He creates on an eternal whim: he is, in the old phrase, *Deus ludens,* the God who *plays.* God blows the bubbles of creation—the shimmering delights that are galaxies and gophers, gamma rays and girls, you, and me, and all things—not because he is sad and needs them to cheer him up or because he is lonely and needs them for company, but because the Persons of the Trinity are already happy in their own company, and therefore free to delight in the mere *happening*—the sheer dumb or wordy *luck*—of their creations. Therefore if God can be said to have any ultimate command at all for his creatures, it can only be that they *be,* not that they behave. Their manners matter less to him than their mere existence. He loves most of all their startling leap out of nothing at the voice of the Beloved. Anything they do after that—good or bad, nasty or nice, forever or for a millisecond—is something he accepts as the price of their being and reconciles to himself by his own holy entrance into their luck.

But that is a much larger subject, to be reserved for later in this book. Time now for

Verses 7-11: on the Beloved's *call* that brings all things out of nothing into being; and on the *dance* by which they always seek to return home to her Bed.

The most startling fact about anybody or anything in the world is not what it is, but *that* it is. To be black or white, male or female, musical or tone-deaf is small potatoes compared with the ability to be at all. But the most fascinating thing about our being is that it is unnecessary. There is no iron rule in the constitution of the universe that says we have to be; there isn't even a rule that says the universe has to be. Rather, there is only the light whim of the

Beloved's call which, at every moment of our existence, beckons us out of nothing and presents us to her Lover. The real thrill of existence is that we almost didn't get on the plane—but then somebody mentioned our name and, by George, here we are in first class.

It's almost impossible to underestimate the consequences of that. For one thing, it means that the being of every single scrap of creation is absolutely fresh at every moment. Whether you are a red giant of a star, or the sphinx, or a mosquito, your *being* is a present, immediate response to the voice of the Beloved—to the creating word of the Wisdom of God. You are not here today because you were here yesterday and are now twiddling your thumbs while you coast downhill back to nothing; rather, you have this very second been brought out of nothing by that voice. Even if you are the oldest thing in the world, and getting more doddering every minute, the act by which you are brought into being, like the act that brings everything else into being, is the newest thing there is. We are all babes when it comes to being; at the roots of our existence it is always Spring.

Unfortunately, our usual way of talking about creation—our habit of referring to it as something that happened *back then* sometime—keeps us from appreciating the freshness of this perception that God makes the whole universe *right now*. Not that there's anything deeply wrong with saying that in the beginning God *made* the world: if the voice of the Beloved calls all things into being at all times, then it called the first things into being at the first time. It's just that confining the idea of creation to the beginning of time and space leaves it too short and too shallow to be any fun. It turns it into a puddle at the front end of the world's driveway instead of an olympic-size pool in the center of the property.

That leads to a second consequence. If the world comes into being out of the play of the divine Lovers—and if it comes out of that play at every moment—then the world at its roots is neither boring, nor somber, nor grim, nor even particularly serious. It is at

this very moment, and at its very core, bright, light, and right—
no matter how cockeyed it may get in its behavior. It is not perched
precariously on the edge of nothing, perpetually afraid of falling
over the cliff. It has just now been tossed triumphantly up out of
the abyss and deposited safe and sound in the sunlight.

Nothing, you see, is good news. For openers, it's God's cup of
tea: in the Bed that is the unity of their Godhead, the Lover and
the Beloved find *nothing* the very thing they were looking for—the
only thing sufficiently open to *all* possibility to suit the freedom
of the loving play by which they create. And for closers, *nothing* is
our cup of tea: far from being threatening or unsafe, it's the very
métier of our existence. Sadly, though, we don't think of it that
way. We live our lives in mortal dread of becoming nothing—of
the dire prospect (as we see it) of simply not being around, say, in
the year 2190. But if you think about that fear, it's as pointless as
it is odd. How many of us spend any time at all fretting about the
fact that we weren't around in 1790? And yet we weren't. Don't
you see? We were nothing once and got bravely over it by the voice
of the Beloved; if the Beloved has further plans to keep whispering
our name to her Lover (which plans, according to the Gospel, she
has assured us of in Jesus), then we shall get bravely over being
nothing as many times as she likes—even world without end.

But there is a third consequence of our being called out of
nothing by her voice that is, if possible, even better than all of the
above. If none of us—not you, not me, not black, not white, not
ducks or geese, not constellations or supernovas—if none of us is
necessary, then all of us are equal. And for one simple reason: *we are
all equally desired, right now, by the divine Lovers.* Every one of us is a
welcome guest at the party they have thrown in their divine Bed.
Try to prove equality on any other basis and it will explode in your
face, fired by the tripwire of unignorable differences. Because we
are not equal. I am a Libra and you are a Virgo; Monique is a genius
and Arthur has the reasoning powers of a rutabaga; kittens are cute
and cockroaches are a catastrophe; and some of us (like my wife)
have yet to find a civilized use for the cocktail hour. But we are all

here because every one of us has been invoked, invited, and included. Our differences are as nothing compared to the equality we share as a result of the Beloved's call.

Verses 12-13: on *home,* and on the *dance.*

We have arrived at the most important single words in my text. The *homing* of the world into the Bed of the divine Lovers is the overarching fact of all existence—the fact of which, one way or another, all other facts are analogues, even sacraments. Take anything you like. Take gravitation, for example. A stone lies seemingly at rest on the ground. In fact, though, it is not at rest at all: precisely because of its *desire,* because of its *love* for the earth, it never ceases to press its way home to the earth. Raise the stone now; lift it six feet off the ground and release it: its resolute haste to go home becomes the most obvious thing in the world. We say it has *weight;* but what it is really heavy with is *desire.* Alternatively, leave it on the ground and dig the soil out from under it: just as resolutely, it continues to hurry home. Or take our lifelong proclivity to return to the womb, or to our childhood's nurturing experiences: it is all a going home. Or take romance: even in its first moment, it is a reawakening of our inveterate hope of finding the home we thought we had lost—and found and lost again and again. Or take even religion: its devices and rituals can never actually bring us home, but it remains a constant witness to the home we are inexorably driven to seek.

We have, of course, always known that. But we have too often stopped short our explanations of it. We trace our desire for home back to the womb, for example; but then we quit there, imagining that when we have arrived at that primal sacrament of home we have arrived at the ultimate explanation of our longing for it. But we haven't. We have simply arrived at another intermediate "because" in a series of "whys" that will not rest until it gets a sufficient, rather than just an interim, answer.

As children, we knew that too. The "whys" of our childhood are endless for a profound reason. Our restless pursuit of an *ultimate* answer—"Why does it rain, Daddy? . . . But why does the sun make water vapor, Daddy? . . . But why is the sun hot, Daddy? . . . But why is there a sun at all, Daddy? . . ."—goes on until somebody gives us an answer to the question left after all the other answers: *"Why is there anything?"* And in the end there are only two possible replies: a vacuous "just because," which is no answer at all; or a firm "God," which is a recognition that if there is an answer, it has to lie somewhere other than in this non-self-explanatory world.

Therefore, to say that we are always trying to go home simply because we started our life here in a home of sorts is no more an explanation of our homing than to say we want to stay alive today because we were alive yesterday. Neither answer addresses itself to the *magnitude* of the desire for home or life, and neither in any way gives us a reason for *approving* of the desire as we so obviously and so heartily do. In the long run, therefore, there are only two views we can take of any question that calls for an ultimate answer: either it matters more than anything else in the world, or it is just so much chin music. There is no middle ground worth talking about.

So to come to the matter of that home toward which my text has all creatures dancing their way—of that Bed from which we came and to which we go: either it's there, or it isn't. Either our desire, all our lives long, to go home—our desire, that is, to go *someplace we will never want to leave again*—is rooted in a home that somehow never left us; or it's just smoke and mirrors—an accidental extrapolation from an assortment of homelike places, not one of which was ever somewhere we wanted to stay. Either the Beloved Wisdom is speaking her sovereign, home-bringing word at the core of our being, or we have spoken it to ourselves. One or the other has to be true. If it is the first, then there *is* a home, even though we deny it; but if it is the second, we are just kidding ourselves, no matter how long or how earnestly we talk about it.

For none of the *sacramental* homes we came from was ever

enough of a home to make us want to stay there. The womb, we left in nine months. Our childhood, we escaped at sixteen or ten, at twenty-four or fifty-three—but whenever it was, it was good-bye and good riddance. Our love affairs, we abandoned regularly. Our marriages (which we tried, with all the sanctions of civil and canon law, to make into an inescapable home), we either left, or pined away in. No home here was ever what we meant by home; yet from birth to death we went on being homesick. So once again, we are back at the same point: either our homesickness is bunk, or it is the greatest thing about us. Either the Beloved has always been calling us home, or home is the final delusion, a creature of air and foxfire that dies in the darkness of our last breath.

We come next therefore to the *dancing* that is the hallmark of our going home. Let me quote from Auden's *Horae Canonicae* (in the section entitled *Compline*):

> Nothing is with me now but a sound,
> A heart's rhythm, a sense of stars
> Leisurely walking around, and both
> Talk a language of motion
> I can measure but not read . . .
> That constellations indeed
> Sing of some hilarity beyond
> All liking and happening. . . .

That's *it,* you see: it is precisely a *party* that draws us to the home at the core of our being. All the motion—and all the emotion— in the world is a dance into the *hilarity,* into the joy, of the Bed that is our origin. That we make wrong moves, that we emote inappro- priately or even wickedly, is all small compared to the freshet of joy at our roots that makes us move or feel at all. "All my fresh springs are in thee," the Psalmist said of Jerusalem; "There lives the dearest freshness deep down things," said Gerard Manley Hopkins. The Ground of our being is not just holy ground, it is fresh and happy ground; it is a garden enclosed, a well of living water, and we go to it gladly. Through all our likings and all our happenings, it is the hilarity beyond them that brings us dancing home.

Verses 14-16: on the *diamond* and on the *happiness* ever after.

I have been borrowing freely so far from one of the great medieval mystics, Meister Eckhart (ca. 1260-1328). My image of the stone in love with the earth, of the Beloved calling to us at the core of our being (Eckhart featured it as the begetting of the Son of God in the soul), and of the homing of creation to the Trinity—all of these are just insights I have lifted (with obvious modifications) from his works. Now at the end of this exposition, however, I am going to shift the locus of my borrowing to a slightly later and (to me) even greater mystic, Dame Julian of Norwich (ca. 1343-1419), the author of *Revelations of Divine Love.* Let me quote for you my main source (from Chapter V of the *Revelations*).

> In this same time our Lord shewed me a ghostly sight of His homely loving. I saw that He is to us everything that is good and comfortable for us: He is our clothing that for love wrappeth us, claspeth us, and all becloseth us for tender love, that He may never leave us; being to us all-thing that is good, as to mine understanding.

> Also in this He shewed me a little thing, the quantity of an hazel-nut, in the palm of my hand; and it was as round as a ball. I looked thereupon with the eye of my understanding, and thought: *What may this be?* And it was answered generally thus: *It is all that is made.* I marvelled at how it might last, for methought it might suddenly have fallen to nought for littleness. And I was answered in my understanding: *It lasteth, and ever shall last for God loveth it.* And so All-thing hath the Being by the love of God.

We have lived for a long time now in a climate of what can only be called astronomical terrorism. The universe, we are told, is such a huge place that we ought to be ashamed of giving ourselves any airs of importance at all. We are little blips on an insignificant planet spinning around a tenth-rate star: what gall, what nerve, to think that our sense of being called home by the voice of some surmised Beloved could matter in the least. The universe probably contains dozens of creatures more or less like us who think similar thoughts: since they (and we) are all equally insignificant, we should just do the universe a favor, shut up about such extravagances, and be content to quake in our negligible boots.

Luckily, the Lady Julian laid such nonsense to rest once and for all six centuries ago: *the universe is no bigger than a nut, but still it matters.* As Chesterton pointed out, size is relative: mere extent doesn't count when you're deciding whether something matters or not. An elephant is bigger than a man; but a man may make a miniature elephant out of ivory and hang it from his watch chain. There is nothing huge and forbidding that cannot, if you shift your perspective a bit, be seen as small and charming—or at least intriguing. And therefore if God can look at the universe and see it as something the size of a hazelnut—or as a diamond no bigger than a peppercorn—we ought to feel free to do the same.

Indeed, it is essential for us to do so if we are to keep our sanity. Think of the question, "Where is God?" And think of how much breath has been wasted on it as a result of accepting the bromide that the universe is a hulking great expanse. People reverently locate God far outside the limits of its vast materiality—and then they have the temerity to wonder why the God they have postulated as "beyond it all" or "above it all" seems so remote and indifferent. But if you turn the image around (as Julian did with her hazelnut and I did with my diamond), the question itself gets turned around. It becomes not, "Where is God?" but, "Where is the universe?" And the answer becomes not, "Far away, beyond all connection" but, "Right there in the Bed of the Trinity, between the thumb and forefinger of the Beloved as she places it in the palm of her Lover."

Do you see the point? That's *friendly;* that's *human;* that's *sane.* It's an answer based on our best, not on our worst. The astronomical terrorists, of course, will continue to object. They will tell you it's merely romantic, or just plain idiotic to talk like that. But they're the idiots. Romance and charm lie a lot closer to the bone of our being than do separation and distance. We spend our lives and our fortunes in pursuit of the happiness we hope for from love and loveliness: why shouldn't we spend the odd intellectual buck on them when we talk about happiness itself? The terrorists, once again, will tell you the whole thing is a delusion: none of it matters when seen against the indifference of their pet monstrosity of a universe. But they're still idiots. If every morning of the year I reject indifference as the proper attitude toward the way my eggs are cooked or my wife smiles, why should I accept it when I talk about where my whole life is going?

So the universe is small—and romantic, and charming, and happy. And the beauty of its loveliness is indeed held forever by the voice of the Beloved. Even sin does not finally have an effect on it. As Jesus said to Julian later in the book (and this time, I give you the original Middle English just for the sheer pleasure of it): *"Synne is behovabil, but al shal be wel & al shal be wel & al manner of thyng shal be wele."* The Beloved, you see, not only *makes* the world by her speaking but she also *restores* it. She brings all things out of nothing by calling their names; and she brings them back from their naughtiness—from their foolish attempts to make themselves nothing again—by re-calling their names. She says "Monique!" and "Arthur!" and presto, you have Monique and Arthur; but when those two make themselves unspeakable by contradicting the speaking of the Beloved—when, in short, they sin (when they are *naughty* in the old, etymological sense of the word)—the Beloved counterspeaks their contradiction at the very moment of its hap- pening and re-calls everything to happiness again.

Let me say here at the end what I really believe. I believe that the incarnation of the Beloved in Jesus is the great sacrament, the effective epiphany of what the Beloved has been doing all along.

Jesus is not to be seen as some appliance-repair specialist in whom the Beloved shows up so she can go from house to house fixing up people who happen to phone in for her services. Jesus is the personal manifestation of the Beloved who *has already respoken the true name of everything in the world*—who has us and all our appliances, however broken, and all our seasons, however mismanaged, right at home with her in Bed—and who already has us totally repaired. That, as I see it, is why salvation—or happiness, to put it in this book's terms—is by faith and not by works. Since the repair job is already done, all you have to do is believe—to trust that it's done—and you're home free; because except for your unbelief, *you were home free already.*

But enough. If you are still wondering what all that has to do with health, money, and love, you will now see: we have finally arrived at the start of this book.

THE COURSE OF THE PURSUIT

Some Observations along the Way

5

Childhood

WHAT I HAVE IN MIND TO DO FROM HERE ON OUT IS TO TAKE a leisurely look at a few of the stages, explorations, and activities involved in our pursuit of happiness—in our lifelong search for the *Home* that creates and reconciles us—and to develop in some detail the themes we've already wrestled with. *Childhood* will be the first stage because it's not only the most definitive sacrament of the Home we seek but also the time of life in which we learn the rudiments of the religions by which we frustrate that search. Next will come *Romance,* which is perhaps our earliest, consciously chosen exploration of the homeward urge—our first realization that the home we have had so far is not our ultimate Home and that we are under a profound compulsion to find some other sacrament of it on our own. After that will come *Vocation* as the day-to-day, down-to-earth activity by which we struggle to create yet another sacrament of Home; and finally, there will be the pursuit of *Well-Being* (with all its subheadings: Food, Fitness, Sport, Sickness, Aging, and Death): in other words, our inveterate quest (and the constant frustrations of that quest) for a liveliness—a quality of life— worthy of the Home we seek.

On with it then, beginning with *Childhood.*

In the history of the race so far, we have survived (more or less) three ways of looking at the mystery of childhood—all of them, naturally, the inventions of adults, and all of them, one way or another, off the mark.

The first had the longest vogue: it lasted from the beginning of recorded thought to the end of the nineteenth century. Children, in this view, were simply little people who had not developed either the brains, the ability, or the willingness to act like big people. Accordingly, its program for dealing with them was twofold: either you waited (patiently, if possible) for them to get over their intractability, or (when you became impatient, as you always did) you beat them to speed up the process of their reform. It didn't much matter what you beat them for. You could do it not only to stop them from doing bad things but also to teach them good things. The forehand wallop, the backhand slap, the cuff on the ears, the bed without supper—these, and worse, were viewed as the sovereign cure for juvenile evil. And the switch across the knuckles or the paddle applied to the backside were likewise seen as the most effective inducements to acquiring anything, be it table manners, Latin verbs, manual dexterity, or musical taste. Not surprisingly, it all worked to a considerable degree, fear being the incentive it is and children being the tough little customers they often are. Indeed, it still does work. Our sensibilities about children may have changed since those days, but our child-rearing practices have not caught up with the changes: even now, there is enough mayhem directed at children to delight even the darkest ages.

Still, that alteration in sensibility did occur, and it was as real as it was extensive. Somewhere toward the end of the reign of

Queen Victoria, a second way of looking at childhood began to develop—a way that did a one-eighty on the subject of the intractability of children. Instead of seeing them as defective adults to be whipped into shape, the post-Victorians took a page from Rousseau and decided that children were actually noble savages— unfallen, wondrous beings in their own right—and that childhood was a magical condition corrupted only by the pressures of adult society. Education (by a false etymology) was to be a *leading out* of all the dandy dispositions already inside the young; drill was to be dropped in favor of letting them set their own program and pace.

It wasn't until the twentieth century, of course, that the practical consequences of this view (less pounding and more persuasion) worked their way into home and school. But by now most of us are to some degree products of it; and to give credit where credit is due, it was definitely an improvement over the outlook it tried to replace. In adopting it, though, we incurred some drawbacks: if we alleviated some of the pressures on children, we didn't seem to do much for their performances. As a matter of fact, we probably lowered them. At this writing, childhood learning is demonstrably down, childhood crime is provably up, and even those of us who survive the system out of jail and in a vocation do less well than our forebears when it comes to keeping a grip on our marriages, our careers, or our sense of direction. Whether the post-Victorian view of childhood actually caused those declines or merely preceded them, I leave for you to decide. Whichever the case, it was the declines themselves—the psychological messes that adults now so frequently find themselves in—that led to the third, and most recent, outlook on childhood.

If I had to give this outlook a name, I would call it the childhood-as-trauma view. To an alarming degree, we now see our formative years as a time when inevitable damage is done—damage we spend the rest of our lives trying to undo. If Johnny had a controlling mother and a distant father, not only do we gloomily expect him to fall for and marry someone who is just as manipulative and remote as his parents were; we are also quite certain that he, and his children, and his childrens' children will keep the same old power struggles and fadeouts going full tilt to the third and fourth generation. Admittedly, we usually allow ourselves some hope that therapy will enable us to be cured of the disease. But even that reliance on therapy has its depressing side. Paradoxically, when the hope of a cure becomes our one and only refuge, we set ourselves up for emotional and philosophical consequences we never counted on.

To be sure, those who undertake therapy can be, and frequently are, helped by it: healing is nothing to sneeze at. But for those who give up on it too soon (or who never get around to it at all), the exaltation of therapy as the great white hope can easily produce little more than anger and depression. As a pastor rather than a therapist—as one who sees not just the select few who opt for treatment but a cross section of the great, gray-green, greasy mass of untreated humanity—I find them generally in one of two postures. If they are not blindly raging against their debilities or lashing out in unfocused resentment at anyone near them, they are slouching along in uncomprehending silence. They are sure that something has gone wrong: the prevalence of the "sickness" view of human nature in general and of childhood in particular has left them in no doubt that they were, and still are, unfairly and disastrously dealt with. But absent any therapy, they haven't a clue as to who is sick (themselves? others? the system? God?) or whom they might properly blame for what. And so, indiscriminately, they blame everybody for everything.

Still, even for those who do seek treatment, the childhood-as-trauma view has drawbacks. It saddles them, in fact, with a larger problem: a philosophical and theological misconstruction of reality. For when you take the view that what you most need is a mopping up of the mess you were deposited in years ago by your "primary caretakers," you set yourself up for the possibility of a whopping error. Not that facing the confusions of your upbringing isn't a useful and salutary enterprise. It is, and nothing I say here is meant to denigrate it. But an unspoken assumption all too easily creeps into your mind: namely, that if you can undo the damage of your early life, all the problems of life itself will be solved and you will then be deposited, without further effort or investigation on your part, in a blissful state. In short, you can easily be led to think that therapy, of itself, can make you happy.

This third view, parenthetically, is a logical consequence of its own reactions to the main features of the first two. From its clear perception of the harm done by the old, beat-the-child-till-he-straightens-out view, it gets its enthusiasm for therapy—for its desire to right the wrongs that derive from being raised by imperfect human beings. But from its endorsement of the post-Victorian view—of the notion that children are fundamentally perfect but for the damage done to them—it has developed the fond notion that the repair of those damages is all that is needed to let the perfection come busting out all over. And if you put those two positions together, you get what most of us now have. You get the idea that somewhere, deep down inside us, there is a kind of unfallen, spontaneous rightness, a hidden garden of hope and fulfillment *needing neither attention nor cultivation*—which, if we could eliminate the weedy overgrowth of childhood neglect and mismanagement, would automatically spring up and surround us like Eden.

But that just isn't true. Therapy, of itself, can't make anybody happy. Happiness is not the absence of unhappy conditions, any more than health is the absence of sickness. You may mend psyches as deftly as you mend broken legs, but unless your patients supply themselves with robust attitudes and actions in their lives, they will soon become sad and sick all over again. Happiness (to say it again) is the ability to take everything that happens and either accept it with delight or reconcile ourselves to it by grace and forgiveness. But we can do that only if we have a conviction that whatever happens is somehow already all right, already reconciled—that (to put it in the terms of the previous chapter, not to mention Rom. 8:28) it has arisen out of a Bed of joy, and that every bit of it is part of a hope-filled call to our home in that Bed. Because even after we are cured of conditions A, B, and C, life goes on happening in all its bright and bewildering variety straight through to the ultimate condition Z of death. Mended hearts and mended legs can break again. Unless you can find some overall way of accepting those breaks (that is, of seeing all luck as holy and therefore safe), your happiness will go right on being held hostage to your dread of bad breaks.

Which brings us, nicely, to childhood as I want to discuss it: not as a condition to be disciplined away, not as a blissful state to be recaptured, and not as damage to be undone, but as the great, first sacrament of the whole mystery of being—of life itself. It is the time when we were given, quite simply, our first lessons in everything. For if life is a school, as I suggested back in chapter three, it is an odd school. Childhood (the school's orientation course, as it were) is not some light once-over designed as little steps for little feet but an all-at-once dumping of every major subject—elementary, intermediate, and graduate-level—into everyone's lap. Health (or sickness), money (or the lack of it), and love (or loneliness, rejection, manipulation, and fear) are in the lesson plan from day one. But more than that, childhood is when we learn all the right and all the wrong responses to make to those subjects. It is when we learn to delight in the breaks of the mystery of our being; and it is when we learn all the religions by which we try to conjure up control over those breaks and substitute plausibilities for the mystery. It is, in short, the foundation course in the theology of being.

To begin with, childhood is our introduction to the most fundamental wonder of creation: the fact that the beginnings of things are so perfectly hidden that the things themselves hardly ever think they began at all. For even though the being of everything arises out of nothing—even though, in the old philosophical phrase, it is created *ex nihilo*—every infant thing, human, animal, or vegetable, quickly comes to the conviction that it has always existed. The act of creation is hidden from creatures. Their physical origin is invisible because they had no developed senses with which to perceive it at the time; and their metaphysical origin is invisible because it's not physical. Plants and animals, of course, presumably never do get around to thinking about that. And if human beings think about it, they do so only after a long period in which they learned the profound lesson that they exist (to use another old phrase) *extra nihil* and *extra causas*—that, astonishingly, they are *outside* nothing and *outside* their causes—that, in short, they are independent beings. This realization begins with children's first cries, and the conviction of it grows more rapidly than anything else about them. To be sure, their being is in fact a gift from others: from their parents, whom they come to recognize early as givers, and from somewhere or someone else (God, in a word) whom they have the option of never recognizing. But at its root, the gift of being remains the best-kept secret in the universe: once a person or a thing exists, all it really experiences of the act of its creation is its independence of that act.

Incidentally, there is often a good deal of loose talk about science being on the verge of discovering the act of creation. We are told that scientists have worked themselves almost back to the point at which they can put their finger on the condition that existed the moment before the first, infinitesimal beginning of the big bang. But that's impossible. Creation will never be a category of science, no matter how long scientists bandy it about. If the universe arises out of nothing by the act of God, then all there can be to discover in the moment before the universe begins is either nothing or God—neither of which, by definition, is discoverable. The secret of creation will always remain a secret as far as science is concerned. The physical sciences can get you all kinds of answers to the question of *what* things are, and it can tell you in detail *how* other things caused them to be what they are. But on the question of *why* they are, the physics department can only be silent. If you want to hear about the ultimate beginning of their beginning, you have to take your chances with the faculties of philosophy and theology.

In any case, children are philosophers before they are scientists: their first thoughtful response to the universe is to assume that it is magic. They love the rabbit from the hat, or the nine yards of scarfs from the closed fist, because at some profound level that sort of thing corresponds with their sense of their own independence of strict causality—with their sense of autonomous being. True enough, they are in fact dependent, both on their parents (for a while) and on God (for good). But when they make their first shopping trip to find a model of the kind of dependence they feel most comfortable with, they choose the one that is furthest removed from *necessary* causation: they opt automatically and eagerly for the magician's unnecessary *word*. They are smart enough, in other words, to realize that the proper first response to creation is astonishment, not explanation. If they are going to admit (as they eventually must) that their independence of their causes is paradoxical—that it is an *independence-in-relationship*—they are still going to insist that the relationship is above all one of wide-eyed wonder, not of narrow necessity.

And that preference for magic over materialism will continue to be the hallmark of all that is best in the subsequent relationships of their lives. Romance (to take just one example) will be the most welcome thing in the world to them because it is precisely an astonishment at the mere being of another person. To be sure, there can be simple, material explanations of how the romantic contraption works: sex drive, perhaps, or the sudden perception of one's parents' patterns (and thus of one's own) in a special someone . . . you name it. But such explanations only describe the road by which you reached the romantic moment, not why you think that moment important enough to risk your life on. And if you ever reach the point of actually preferring such reductionism over your native astonishment—if you opt for materialism instead of magic as the correct explanation of your being— you will lose the love of risk-for-the-sake-of-wonder you first learned in childhood. And your relationships themselves will be reduced to little more than exercises in cost accounting.

Nowhere is that better illustrated than in childhood's other profound astonishment: children are utterly fascinated by luck. They delight in the arbitrariness of the way the world runs, and until they develop (early on, alas) a desire to control its changes and chances, they enjoy something very like the state of Adam and Eve before the fall.

Let me put in one demurrer here. Since I am about to use the story of the Garden of Eden as a reference point, you should know that I refuse to rule out either of its two major interpretations. For my money, it can be taken (though not necessarily in all its literal details) as the story of the human race's earliest historical experience with this chancy world; or it can be taken as the story of your, and my, and everybody's encounter with that same world *in our own lives.* If I lean a bit more heavily here on the second reading, don't think I have ruled out the first.

Like Adam and Eve, children find themselves in a world where everything is a matter of luck. They didn't arrange for their presence in it: they simply woke up one day and found themselves inexplicably *there.* And they didn't do anything to shape its character. Adam and Eve didn't design the animals or the trees, they named them. They said, "Holy cow! That's not an ox, that's a wildebeest!" or more darkly, "Hey, that tree can make us wise, even though we're not supposed to eat from it." Like children, they initially found the world something to play with in astonishment; only after that did they think of trying to control it. Games were their first love: the luck of the draw was quite sufficient to keep them delighted. Cheating ("We'll be like gods"—the wilful effort to put body English all over an otherwise delightful game) and lying about the cheating ("It's not the eating we feel guilty about, it's our nakedness") came second. But the cheating and the lying were more than sufficient to spoil the game. The fall occurred early enough in the story of the race to corrupt the rest of history, and it occurs early enough in everyone's childhood to corrupt the rest of our lives.

That's one reason, I think, why there are two creation stories in the Book of Genesis. The first one (Gen. 1:1–2:3—the seven-day account) simply lays out the game with all the gorgeous chanciness of its givens. But perhaps because that was too rosy to explain the mess the world is in, the Holy Spirit felt it necessary to include the second account (Gen. 2:4–3:24—the Garden of Eden story). In the race's childhood as well as in our own childhoods there was a game; but there was also something in each that went wrong with the way we played the game. It wouldn't do to talk about the one without the other.

Enter here, therefore, the subject of *original sin*—or, as it is more accurately called in Latin, *vitium ex origine:* the defect, the sickness, from our beginning. Why do I bring up such an old, complicated subject? Because we have gotten ourselves into an old, complicated situation. You can't say simply that we are good, any more than you can say that we are nothing but bad. What you have to say is that we took the marvelous luck of our origin—the luck that in every one of its ramifications, convenient or inconvenient, was all holy—and somehow violated its holiness. We cheated; and worse yet, we developed a preference for cheating. But even at that, the game was never cancelled nor was our ability to delight in it ever quite eclipsed. We are good *and* bad: good, by the creative breaks given us through the divine will and through our own willingness to play along with them, and bad by our ham-handed jimmying of those breaks right from the start.

Take, for example, a simple, children's card game my grandfather taught me—a game called, "Drive Your Neighbors out of Doors." To play it, you first split the pack evenly between yourself and your opponent. Then each of you holds his own cards face down in a stack and takes turns laying one card at a time, off the top, on a pile between the two of you. If a card from ten down turns up, you simply keep on alternating laydowns; but if you happen to turn up a picture card, your opponent has to cover it by laying on additional cards: four on an Ace, three on a King, two on a Queen, and one on a Jack. And if, in the process of doing that, your opponent should turn up a Queen as, say, her third card against your Ace, you must then try to beat her Queen by turning up a face card of your own in not more than two tries. If you fail to do so, your opponent picks up the whole stack on the table, puts it on the bottom of her pack, and the game continues until one of you takes all of the other's cards. Obviously, "Jacks are the boys," as my grandfather used to say: when a Jack is laid on the pile, your opponent has only one chance to cover your card.

Now think of the typical child's reaction to that game. In the beginning (ex origine), it is unvarnished delight in the luck of it all: the thrill of just seeing what happens, the *happiness* that only a chancy world can give. But then three other possibilities suggest themselves. The first is the itch to cheat by peeking at the next few cards on the top of your deck. The child wants to be God, knowing the future—knowing what the luck of the draw will be rather than accepting it when it comes. The second is darker: she slips a Jack to the bottom of her pack so that when she comes to her last card she will have more of a chance to beat her opponent. But the third is darkness itself: she slips several Jacks to the bottom and, having memorized the location of the face cards in her opponent's hand, she deals the Jacks off the bottom at the crucial times. She has become what she wanted to be: God. Not the real God, of course; because except for the odd miracle poked in here and there as a sign, God doesn't interfere like that in the luck of the world's draw. But she has become at least a god, knowing good and evil: the good that was once the game, and the evil of her wrecking of the game by refusing to play it without cheating.

Do you see? Hers is the story of the whole human race: to avoid being losers, we have lost the game itself. The earth is holy ground because it is lucky ground, because the free interactions of its occupants were designed to produce a happy game—a rough-and-tumble ecology in which a delicate yet monumental balance could be sustained. But for all of our history (and devastatingly so in this century) we have fiddled with the luck and all but obscured the holiness. There is, of course, a profound sense in which the holiness is indestructible. Even if we fry the earth in a nuclear holocaust and freeze it in a sunless winter of radioactive fallout, it will still reach its own holy balance: a new, if dire, version of the ecology will simply replace the old, kindly one. But we ourselves will be out of the game: even the meek will not inherit that earth; only the rocks and the cockroaches will.

But that gets us ahead of the story. Childhood remains the time in which we learn not only the game but also the way to destroy the game—in which we both discover and forget how to *play.* Let me end this chapter, therefore, with some observations on just how central play is, not only to childhood but to the whole created order.

First of all, as I've already noted, God *plays* when he makes the world. He does not dictate the actions of creatures; he tosses them off and lets them do their own thing. I have very little patience with people who rattle on about the Divine Plan—who talk as if God had the script of history already written and all we had to do was find a copy and stick to it, or else. . . . If God can be said to have a plan at all, it is probably much more like street theater, or improvisational drama, than like the drill-team exercises such people imagine. He is not a martinet of a director who can put on a show only if the weather or the actors are doing exactly what is printed on his pages. Things and people can do whatever they want and he can still make a play of it. They can even (according to the Gospel) conspire to murder the Divine Director himself and still not spoil the happy ending he brings out of the dumb luck of his death and the great good luck of his resurrection.

But more than that, *play* is built into the very natures of the creatures he brings into being. And even though you may think it whimsical of me, I am going to insist that he builds it into all creatures, mineral, vegetable, or animal. Rocks play in a dance with the earth itself—in their ponderous love affair with it that we call gravitation (remember Eckhart!). Tomato plants play when they snake their hairlike roots down around stones in their amorous pursuit of water. And animals? Well, even you will have to concede that the higher up the ladder of creation you go, the more playful the creatures become.

For the fascinating truth is that the more developed the creature, the less able it is to cope with the world until it has played with it. A mountain, the moment it is a mountain, is fully equipped to be mountainous: it hardly needs to play at all. A mustard plant has to fool around a bit more (with soil, sunlight, water, air) before it can be properly mustardy. But a mouse, or a macaw, or a Maine coon cat, or a management consultant—these have to play a great deal before they can manage anything. It's as if the Creator had computers in mind when he made the higher creatures: the more powerful the hardware of the model, the more dependent it is on software—and on self-developed software at that. Consider only the top-of-the-line model. When a baby is born, there are only a handful of activities it comes factory-set to run: it can breathe, suck, swallow, and respond to loud noises and sudden withdrawal of support. All the rest of the programs it needs—nursing, crawling, walking, talking, whistling, reading, whittling, romancing—it acquires through play. A horse can stand almost the minute it is foaled; but human beings take their own sweet time about that and about everything else.

But the Creator had more than computers in mind when he made us. There is one thing no computer, however powerful or however programmed, will ever do: turn itself on out of its own sheer pleasure and show you something. The highest form of play is precisely *turning ourselves on in order to turn others on;* it is the offering up of the good *in delight, for delight.* And that kind of play, while it does not occur at the very start of childhood, still begins so early that there aren't many of us who can remember the first time we held out a bright yellow ball for our mother's inspection. We are playful offerers of creation almost from square one because we are meant to be playful offerers of it all the way up to square forever. Adam offered up the animals by naming them, and he offered up Eve by falling for her as bone of his bones and flesh of his flesh. He and we, you see, are nothing short of *priestly* beings, *offerers* of creation to each other and to God. And while priesthood may have gotten a bad name in the time between him and us, our inveterate bent for offering remains the biggest, most playful thing about us. We are always turning ourselves on. And we are always, until we are dead or cynical, trying to turn others on as well. What is romance but that? What is playing the flute but that? What is cooking *Tripe Niçoise* for company but that? It is all *play inviting others into play.* We are never more fully human than when we do it; and we are never less so than when we don't. The *less,* of course, is the story of our fall. But the *more* remains what we are all about.

6

Childhood: More

WE NEED TO TALK A BIT MORE, HOWEVER, ABOUT THIS EARLY childhood fall from priestliness and play. One of the things we lost when we stopped viewing children as little sinners and saw them instead as budding saints or hapless victims was an answer to the question of what's wrong with us—an answer, specifically, that didn't in the same breath deny what's right about us. The great advantage of the doctrine of original sin as an explanation of the predicament of our priestliness was that it never pretended there was any way we could escape from either the good of our priestly nature or the evil that inevitably results from our failed exercise of it. On the one hand, original sin did indeed say that right from the start of our lives there was something incurably wrong with us, to wit, that we were somehow profoundly unable (not just occasionally unwilling) to make the playful offerings of reality we were designed to make. But on the other hand, when the doctrine was correctly expounded, it still insisted not only that we were designed as offerers but that we remain under an inescapable compulsion to fulfill that design. We are not simply a mass of perdition with no vestiges of our original nature. We have all of our original nature, and we quite rightly go on trying to exercise it. Our problem is not that we are unadulteratedly bad, but that we can never quite manage to be unadulteratedly good. In short, we are prone to both goodness and badness at the same time.

If that strikes you as improbable, let me give you an analogy from the phenomenon of partial red-green color blindness (I am both a sinner and color-blind, so I can speak as an expert on either subject). To begin with, both my inability to avoid sin—to avoid the perversion of my priesthood—and my inability to tell certain reds and greens apart are *defects from my beginning,* not accidents that happened to me along the way. They are both of them due to equipment that malfunctioned as soon as it functioned at all. They are not just the result of imperfect training by others or wilful impairment by myself. I do not offer up my world perversely just because my parents set me bad examples of offering or because I refused for my own reasons to learn how to offer. Even if I had been raised with perfect examples, I would still not be free of my propensity to make shabby offerings; and even if I had the best intentions in the world, I would still not be able to implement them perfectly. Likewise, I do not fail to distinguish red from green because I was taught my colors wrong or because I refused to take corrective measures. Both my original sin and my color blindness, you see, are uncorrectable conditions. They would be with me now no matter how I was taught or how hard I worked to overcome them. I am radically incurable on either count.

Nevertheless, just as partial color blindness does not prevent me from seeing a great deal of the world of color, so original sin by no means prevents me from making, at times and in places, wonderful and humanity-fulfilling offerings. I am no more a totally depraved offerer than I am a total nonperceiver of color. But I can never quite trust myself in either department—and I can easily make whopping errors in both.

As a child, for example, I learned early on that there was something radically undependable about the way I saw colors. I could go along for weeks correctly identifying what I saw: all the yellows and blues, and even a good many of the reds and greens. But there always came a time when my nasty little cousins from Jersey would catch me out. They played a guessing game, the rules of which they always explained by saying (in the idiom of their New Jersey childhood), "I must tell you a color, and you must tell me what I'm thinking of." I remember in particular a day on which one of them said, "I see something gray; what is it?" I looked around, saw a gray sedan parked across the street, and promptly said, "That car over there!" Their response? Gales of derisive laughter. The car, of course, was green.

The rest of my life has been a series of such misadventures: appearing at a party wearing a red Christmas tie with a salmon shirt because I thought the shirt was off-white; greeting a hostess's lime pie with, "I just love raspberry chiffon!" and so on, into a long career of equally colorful mistakes.

But the undependability of my color-perceiving equipment is a trifle compared with the unpredictable breakdowns I have had to put up with when it comes to my priestly nature. I have set out to love people and found I was only using them. I have sworn myself to major delight in a subject and discovered I was indulging in little more than minor amusement. I have vowed faithfulness to an enterprise and watched my fidelity founder on the rocks of the first inconvenience. And in all of this, it was as useless for me to promise not to make such mistakes in the future as it would have been to swear never again to mistake red for green or aqua for blue. I might, of course, have tried to be more cautious—to make only safe, paltry offerings or to settle for a wardrobe of nothing but clerical black-and-white. But since that would have amounted to less than living in the one case, and been less than interesting in the other, I never did it. Even with defective equipment, I was still as bound and determined to offer as I was bound and determined to see color. It might have been safer not to have to say I'm sorry so often; but when human push came to priestly shove, I, like almost everybody else, chose rather to be sorry than safe.

We are, of course, in the habit of thinking that this predicament is the most normal thing in the world. But one of the other benefits of the doctrine of original sin is an insistence that our failed priestliness isn't normal at all—that it is in fact the most peculiar thing in the world and that it is strictly limited to human beings. The rest of creation—mineral, vegetable, or animal—doesn't seem in the least liable to original sin. Even the beasts of the field that are closest to us on the staircase of creation are not beastly in the ways we can be. They survive their upbringing without becoming sinners and without having to pretend they are either saints or victims. They make their juvenile mistakes, of course, and they take their lumps for them; but they suffer no *vitium* from their *origine*. Their mothers cuff them around when they are nuisances and kick them out of the nest before they are ready; but they don't develop our kinds of hang-ups over their upbringing. Within the confines of their several natures, they make their offerings of themselves and of their world in ways that fulfill rather than violate their natures. Only we manage to undo ourselves when we try to be ourselves. Only we are unnatural.

That is perhaps the main point of the story of Adam and Eve in Genesis. Their fall did *not* involve doing something that came naturally to them. It was not that they discovered something about themselves which, once discovered, became a curse. It was not, *pace* all the prurient interpretations of the story, that they fell into a booby trap called sexuality and became victims of a divine bad joke. No, all creatures above a certain level discover sexuality; and they find it not a trap but the enjoyable, if slightly confusing, thing it really is. Rather, Adam and Eve—and all of us in our several lives—went a million miles out of the way to discover something that wasn't there at all. They found a reason to offer up the world that addressed not *what the world was* but *what it could be made to be in some other scheme of things than its own.* Instead of matter, they opted for meaning— and for alien, dead-wrong meaning at that. The tree would make them wise. They would be as gods, knowing good and evil.

Do you see how unnatural that was? As far as knowing good

was concerned, there was nothing but good for them to know. And as for knowing evil, there simply wasn't any around. They had to *invent* it. And we go right on having to invent it as well. Because all things, insofar as they exist at all, are good. They are every last one of them—cancer cells, blood parasites, and loan sharks included—responses to the creative act of God, to the delight by which the Beloved speaks them into being for her Lover's good pleasure. There is no *ontological* evil anywhere in the world. The only way you can drag evil into the act is to take some good and offer it up the wrong way—to try to know the good *in contradiction* to what the Beloved Word really says about it. The world of evil, therefore, is actually a perverse creation, a parallel universe of air and darkness that has no God-given reality at all. But (and this is the biggest *but* in the world) because that weird, unnatural universe so preoccupies the human race—because we spend so much of our real, God-given energy making offerings to that fake world—evil does indeed acquire power over reality. *We* become its agents. *Through us,* it warps the world itself.

Which brings us, once again, to the subject of religion. Let me play my cards face up here. I am going to maintain that the principal device by which original sin works—the main activity by which it gets its power and produces its results—is religion. And if you will be kind enough to remember all the things I said in my earlier chapters about using the word in an admittedly unusual way—about using it to refer not to particular, historic religions but to the human race's proclivity for conjuring with the real world on the basis of an essentially unreal scheme of things—I will get on with the job at hand.

There is a simple reason why religion is the principal device by which original sin works: original sin, being a general breakdown of human priestliness, leads us to hunt frantically for some substitute priestly activity that will be exempt from the breakdown—for an activity we will be able to bring off despite the breakdown. And that hunt is what leads us straight to religion; because religion, as a closed, arbitrary system, is by definition immune from the vicissitudes of the real world. But the path by which religion comes to involve itself with priestly activity is a bit more complicated to trace, because priesthood is not exclusively or even primarily a religious category. The business of lifting up things (and people) into higher unities—into further, more elaborate moves in the Dance of Creation—is something we do by nature, constantly. Beginning with our primitive ancestors, for example, generations of gardeners have lifted vegetables into ever higher forms. The variety and perfection of the produce we now have is the result not just of random development but of centuries of loving, priestly attention to what the original vegetables were and to the further exaltations of which they might be susceptible. Likewise, and even more clearly, generations of cooks have lifted vegetables higher still. An eggplant is wonder just sitting in the garden; but give it the benefit of culinary, priestly regard and it can enter into civilization—into the City of Creation—as Ratatouille, as Imam Bayeldi, as Caponata, as Eggplant Parmigiana . . . as, literally, any eggplanty thing you can name.

But as the doctrine of original sin points out, the history of this natural, human priesthood has been a mixed proposition. On the one hand, our priestliness has lifted many things well: the crafts, the arts, and the sciences are not things you find lying about in the wild; they are priestly exaltations of natural phenomena into the higher unities of the City. On the other hand, just as much or even more of our priestly lifting has perverted rather than exalted nature. We have offered up animals in cruelty, human beings as slaves, the young of every generation in war, and the whole ecology of the earth as if it were a disposable diaper.

Perhaps now you see why religion so readily involved itself with priesthood. Quite rightly, it saw that what had gone wrong with the world was the result of a perversion of human priestliness. And just as correctly, it saw that the righting of the wrong would have to involve the restoration of our priesthood to its integrity. But when religion cast about for some way of accomplishing that restoration, it found itself confronted with the monumental obstacle described by the doctrine of original sin: our priesthood was so deeply compromised that there was nobody in the world who could be counted on not to make perverse offerings. And so religion, despairing of ever straightening up the historical offerings in the real world, opened up an alternative priestly shop in a parallel world—in a world *next door to history*—where religion itself would make the rules of offering and then simply decree (on no particular evidence) that if the rules of that parallel world were observed, the troubles of the real world would be resolved. It developed, in short, a recipe for action in the world next door to history that would supposedly straighten up every situation in the historical world. Had you murdered your brother? Sacrifice an ox. Were your enemies at the gates? Fast for a week. Were cutworms destroying your tomato crop? Offer money to the temple. Was the Dance of Creation a disaster? Stand on the sidelines and jump up and down.

That, you see, is the fundamental trouble with religion: as far as real life is concerned it is always on the sidelines. It is *over there,* trying to stave off disaster by making irrelevant offerings in some arbitrary world, while the disastrous offerings in the real world go on just as before. It is a parallel dance that has no necessary, beneficial effect on the actual Dance of Creation. Worse yet, it can also become a tyrannical dance that in fact adds to the disasters of the real Dance. Accordingly, if we now try to specify the devices by which religion perpetuates the damage of original sin, we will be able to list them as the perversions of priesthood they actually are.

- First of all: religion operates in a self-originated, parallel world rather than in the world as originated by God.

- Second: because the world it thus confects exists only inside us, it operates by directing our attention and our efforts to our own insides rather than to the world we actually inhabit.

- Third: it makes the false assumption that these pseudo-priestly, internal transactions we busy ourselves with have some controlling effect on the outside world.

- And fourth: because it thus neglects to concern itself with the transactions of actual history, it encourages and compounds the disasters that already flow from our failure to make true priestly offerings of the real world.

. But rather than illustrate these perversions of priesthood with random examples, let us now kick back and for the rest of this chapter take a longish look at some of the specific ways we fall into them in our early childhood experiences with the three main subjects of this book—with Health, Money, and Love.

Health is not the absence of sickness; it is the normal, positive condition of every natural organism—a condition the organism sustains, unless interfered with, simply because it is designed to do so. Accordingly, no one needs to *induce* health by special measures; if you simply take suitable care of the organism, the organism will take care of its health. Sickness, however, *is* an induced condition—one caused by something genetic, infectious, or parasitic that adventitiously interferes with the nature of the organism.

Admittedly, there is plenty of sickness in the world, especially in childhood. In addition to the fact that all children can suffer diseases ranging from the common cold to spinal meningitis, many of them enter the world sick or deformed. Children are born with AIDS, with cocaine addiction, with spinabifida, or with a host of other afflictions. Nothing I say here is meant to minimize the horror of such conditions. I only want to point out that we would not even recognize those conditions as sickness if we did not have some prior assessment of what constitutes a healthy human child.

That prior assessment, however, is the very thing that is most imperiled by the pseudo-priestly offerings we make when it comes to health—by the religions of health we so easily and so early embrace. Take, for example, the subject of the transmissibility of disease. There is a powerful inclination, both on the part of the adults who talk about the subject and the children who listen, to subscribe to bogeyman theories of health and sickness. My four-year-old grandson, Andrew, is extremely conscious of what he calls "germs." If the peanut butter sandwich I am making for him falls on the floor of my kitchen, he refuses to eat it because it has become contaminated with germs. If his brother sneezes on him, he has come under lethal attack from germs. Everyone else seems to take his attitude as quite normal; I see it as a prime example of the abnormality I have called original sin.

The whole subject of germs, as he deals with it, is a perfect instance of a parallel universe. True enough, there are microorganisms of all kinds in the real world and many of them can make mischief, sometimes serious mischief. And true enough again, there are often prudent steps to be taken to combat the mischief: vaccinations, for example, or tetanus shots, or the cleansing of wounds. But my grandson's behavior is not based on such prudential considerations. Instead, it is based on a fascination with evil and disaster—on what I am tempted to call the Six-O'clock-News approach to health. Think of the unreal, sensationalist world Andrew inhabits. First, the conspiracy theory of history reigns supreme in that world. Germs have all the power and they are lying in wait everywhere to get him. Health is not a strong, positive condition in which his body naturally repulses such insidious forces; it is a fragile, precarious condition in which they are able to wreak havoc at will. He lives not in the real world but in a parallel universe beset by biological warfare: the enemy has the upper hand at all times.

Second, this parallel world is a hothouse not only of paranoia but of religion. Because the enemy is invisible, it is impossible for my grandson simply to trust anyone, even those closest to him, not to do him harm; he must make ritual sacrifices to insure his safety. If he has the sniffles, he must abstain from kissing his baby sister. If his peanut butter sandwich picks up even a single dog hair, it is not enough that his grandfather remove the hair; the entire sandwich must be immolated to keep the enemy from the gates.

Third, even though he is convinced that all of this religiosity is absolutely true and necessary, the parallel world it substitutes for his real environment is actually a tissue of half-truth and downright falsehood. My kitchen floor is not necessarily host to more germs than anyplace else, and it almost certainly harbors fewer of them than his own hands. Furthermore, for the vast majority of his hours and days, most germs that do surround him are ones he has either defeated outright or negotiated an easy peace with.

But fourth and most important, despite the paranoia, the frantic religiosity, and the manifest silliness of his parallel universe, he not only accepts it as true; he goes gladly out of his way so to accept it. Please be clear about what I am saying here. I am not saying that "germs" are negligible forces; and I am certainly not maintaining that there is no place in the real world for such things as antiseptics, antibiotics, or keeping open cuts clear of blood contaminated by the AIDS virus. Nor am I holding simply that his mother and father have inculcated his fear of germs by faulty and alarmist instruction. By and large, in fact, I think they have been fairly sensible in what they have told him. What I am really saying is that he (and any other member of the human race, young or old) is somehow disposed to credit the parallel universe more readily than the real one.

This goes back to what I said earlier when I maintained that original sin is not just a matter of bad training, but a positive and eager preference for the false world rather than the true. Other instances besides enthusiastic germ-phobia abound in childhood. A good many children live in rather pleasant worlds—in worlds that are not in fact filled with horrors; yet all children more readily believe (and are fascinated by) tales of horror than tales of good. Or to take another instance, some children are even given sane and loving instruction about sexuality; yet no child gets very far past his or her fifth birthday without developing a conviction that sex is somehow dirty—or at the very least, a subject for sniggers.

It is not enough to write off this proneness to dwell on evil rather than good as due simply to faulty nurture, or to the pressure of tiny peers. It is more than that. It is a positive delight—a fascination, in each and every child of Adam and Eve, with evil. It is, in short, original sin; and it leads straight to a preference for religious, rather than real, attempts to deal with the world. It leads, as I have said, to the construction of a parallel world in which ritually defined evils threaten continually to destroy everything unless they are expiated by religious acts.

Perhaps the clearest instance of this religionizing tendency in childhood is to be found in one other health-related subject, namely, the matter of food. The human race is at least as religious about what it eats as it is about anything else; and there is probably no topic on which children are given more catechetical lectures than on diet. Think of the creedal structures we constantly erect around their eating habits: chicken soup cures colds; spinach makes you strong; leaving Brussels sprouts on your plate hurts children in Africa; and, of course, salt will kill you, butter is bad for you, vegetables are better than meat, and fish will make you smart. But it isn't just that the idiotic content of the catechism corrupts them; it's that they themselves, quite apart from any specific indoctrination, are more than ready to be indoctrinated. If they are not taught religions about food, they will invent them. Even left quite on their own they will decide, for example, that the sliminess of cooked onions is a death threat, or that green peas are unsafe unless embedded in mashed potatoes. Like the rest of us, you see, they are religious creatures—victims of original sin—and never more so than when it comes to food. They will buy dietetic mumbo jumbo and ritual eating habits far more readily than they will taste an actual piece of Stilton or a given dish of braised fennel. They will propitiate the gods of what is on their plates sooner than they will pay attention to the food itself. They will, in short, look *in* at the parallel world more easily than they will look *out* at the real one.

But enough for the moment about Health. Think next of Money as an illustration of the religionizing tendencies of childhood. Since this is the first time in this book the subject has come up at any length, let me begin with a definition.

Money is an immaterial system of parameters for defining or expressing value. Just as we use feet and inches to define length, pounds and ounces to define weight, and calories to define the amount of heat given off in burning, so we use dollars, marks, francs, or yen to define value. But be careful to note the word *immaterial* in that definition: ounces, inches, calories, and dollars are not things, they are measurements. I can give you a 10-ounce steak, for example, but I cannot give you 10 ounces *tout court.* I can give you a tablespoonful of olive oil and assure you it will produce 90 calories worth of heat, but I cannot give you just 90 calories. And likewise, I can give you a $1.49 package of supermarket cookies, or a single $1.49 designer cookie from a gourmet bake shop, but I cannot give you $1.49.

I realize that this last assertion startles you. You're thinking to yourself, "Of course he could give me $1.49: all he'd need would be a one-dollar bill, a quarter, two dimes, and four pennies—or maybe a personal check for the amount. Pounds and calories may be immaterial; but doesn't he know that money—in the form of bills, coins, and credit instruments—actually exists?" Well, think again. Because when you do, you will quickly realize that you need to make a theological distinction when you talk about money. Bills, coins, and checks are not themselves money; they are rather *sacraments* of money—outward and material signs of the immaterial set of parameters that money really is by my definition. (Sacraments, incidentally, are defined in the Book of Common Prayer as "outward and visible signs of inward and spiritual grace"; change *spiritual* to *immaterial,* and *grace* to *value,* and you've got money as a sacrament.)

There was a time, of course, back in what are usually called the good old days, when the immateriality of money was not as obvious as it is now—when the sacramental instruments of money (gold coins, for example) were themselves objects of value. But you must remember that even back then, the value of those instruments *as money*—that is, what they were actually worth in terms of what they could buy—still fluctuated in response to the fluctuations of the marketplace. In any case, all of that is now just grist for the nostalgia mill: monetary instruments nowadays are totally sacramental—so much so that money is probably the most spiritual thing in most people's lives. Between the checks, the plastic cards, the Federal Reserve Notes, and the coins made out of God knows what, our entire material life is defined and conducted by means of an immaterial system that operates through arbitrary sacramental signs—that is, by means of something awfully close (in principle at least) to an immaterial, parallel universe.

We actually do, you see, live in two worlds at once. There is the material world of your living-room furniture, for example, and there is the immaterial world of money that you did business in to acquire the furniture. In the material world, for example, you own a recliner: it is yours to sit in or spill beer on as you like. In the immaterial world, however, you don't own the chair; the god VISA owns it until you have made the required number of ritual sacrifices. But the real giveaway of the secret of trade—the tipoff as to which of the two worlds you live in is actually the governing world—comes when something goes wrong in one or the other of them. If the mistake should happen to be of your doing—if you default, say, on the sacrifices the religion of money insists you must make in order to go on owning your recliner—your dearly loved beer-scented, nacho-encrusted Monday Night Football companion will go straight out of your life, sucked inexorably back into the parallel universe of money. But if what goes wrong is the parallel universe's fault—if your recliner's footrest breaks, perhaps—that's another story. Have you tried getting something fixed these days? Especially something under warranty—something, that is, still supposedly under the rules that insure fair play between the two universes? Well, the parallel universe has a surprise for you. There are, it seems, two rules it hasn't told you about—rules that it invokes every time you try to get it to do something in the real world. The first is that it will make it as difficult as possible for you to get your merchandise to one of its customer service temples (they are invariably located where you are not: there is probably no one in the world who lives anywhere near a Sears repair center). And the second is that if and when your merchandise does get into the temple, the parallel universe will not let it out until you have made further and more extraordinary ritual offerings: fourteen phone calls (of up to thirty rings each because nobody even bothers to answer), two letters (enclosing copies of the sales slip to prove date of purchase), and one personal appearance at the temple (because they can't find your letters and are not allowed to take your word for anything over the phone).

Now you might think that it would be difficult to take ordinary, material human beings and get them to accept such nonsense as having any place in the real world. But it isn't. Beginning early in childhood, the religion of money—which is what gives this whole immaterial scheme of things its power to define our values—is assiduously, if more or less unconsciously, inculcated in us.

I think it's safe to say that no child is ever given money without some careful indoctrination into the religion of money. We may occasionally manage to loosen up enough on the religion of food to give children ice cream, for example, just for the fun of it— without making them recite the latest catechism on cholesterol. But give them *money* just for the fun of it? Never. Money isn't funny. It's a solemn subject and must never be handed around without all the reverences and genuflections due the Holy. In fact, I would even go so far as to say that it is in connection with money that children first acquire their sense of the awe that the Holy is supposed to evoke. They may be instructed how to say their prayers to God, or how to conduct themselves when receiving Holy Communion; but in no case is the need for reverence, for seriousness of purpose, and for the careful watching of every step better taught than when they are given their first dimes, quarters, or dollars.

Refresh your sense of what really goes on. Imagine first that you give three-year-old Arthur a grape. He looks at it, puts it in his mouth, rolls it around a few times, and then spits it halfway across the room. You might be tempted, of course, to give him a lecture on the religion of food ("That's *food,* Arthur; you shouldn't fool around with it when people are starving"). But on the other hand, you might find Arthur's grape shooting as funny as he did and, realizing that fooling around with food is precisely the way all great cuisines got to where they are, you might just smile and offer to show him your trick of removing the peel from an orange in one long strip.

But now imagine that you give Arthur a five-dollar bill for his birthday and that after he has extracted it from the card, he tears it in half. At that moment, of course, no one in the room (maybe not even little Arthur) has any clear notion of why he tore the bill. Maybe he hates you. Maybe he's trying to be funny. Maybe he thinks it's Monopoly money. My point is that all of a sudden, it doesn't matter that you find out what his motives are. Everybody in the room will react exactly as if the Sacrament had been profaned. And their reaction will be the most effective religious instruction Arthur will ever get because it will proceed not out of their intellect or their feelings but out of the very core of their faith. What they have just seen done is not something they think is merely a poor idea, or a naughty thing to do. It is not even something that *ought not* to be done. All those formulations of their reactions are too mild to express what they really believe. What they have seen is something that *must not* be done, that *cannot be done*—something that comes so close to pulling the linchpin of reality that it is unthinkable and intolerable—something, in short, that can only be called sacrilege and blasphemy.

The difference, you see, between Arthur's shooting of the grape and his rending of the five-dollar bill is that in the case of the money, there is just no way that the onlookers could avoid giving the religion lecture—or that Arthur, on his side, could avoid learning what blasphemy really means. So much so, that I will give you a little experiment to help you realize just how early this totally effective instruction in the religion of money gets into children's souls. The next time you are at a large family gathering—one with children of all ages, from toddlers, through two- and three-year-olds, through fives, sevens, nines, and so on up—get everyone's attention and then quietly, with no explanation, light up a cigar with a twenty-dollar bill. And as you let the bill burn completely before dropping it in the ash tray, watch everyone's reactions. From the children who are two years old and under you will get no religious reaction, just whatever attention they give to someone holding a flaming paper in his hand. But you will probably get mystified looks from the three-year-olds in the room; and by the time you get as high as the fives, you will see the alarm and confusion that attends real blasphemy. You will see faces that have looked on something that threatens to end a world.

If you in any way grasp the depth and the panic of that feeling, you will begin to see why the only sufficient response to blasphemy has traditionally been to kill the blasphemer—an option which, for your sake, I hope your family will avoid. But, if you have also grasped what I've been saying about the religion of money and the parallel universe that is its true homeland, you will see just as clearly that the world actually threatened by your blaspheming of the twenty-dollar bill is not this world at all but rather the parallel one: not the world of things but the immaterial system of parameters by which we allow money to define things.

True enough, your family's first admonitions after you have burned the twenty will seem to be about things rather than money. After they have assured themselves that the blasphemy has actually occurred ("You mean that *wasn't* a fake twenty?") they will try to convince you of the error of your ways by arguing that destroying a "real" twenty has deleterious effects on people and things. Totally ignoring the fact that *all* twenties are fakes—creatures of the immaterial, parallel universe—they will insist that this recently incinerated one could have made a great material difference. They will say, "That's a waste!" or, "That could have been put to good use!" or, "You could have saved it for a rainy day!" or, "How could you do such a thing in a world full of hungry people?" But all the while, the head of emotional steam behind their remonstrances is created almost entirely by their religious conviction that you have profaned the Holy. They will sum up their case, therefore, by reminding you that the temple police—the Federal authorities—could very well come after you as a criminal.

To help you answer them, here are some possible responses to their badgering.

- *To the charge of waste:* Pat your wallet and say, "I have more where that came from."

- *To the challenge to find a better use:* Pull out your checkbook and say, "Name me a charity and I'll write out a contribution."

- *To the rainy-day argument:* Throw up your hands and say, "Listen, if I was living only to take care of rainy days, I would have fed you all tuna casserole, not rib roast and wild rice."

- *To the hungry-people ploy:* Go to the pantry and give them twenty dollars' worth of canned creamed corn to wrap up as care packages.

- *But to their warning that the Feds will get you:* Draw yourself up straight and say, "Aha! Now why, I wonder, would they do that? Why would the temple police arrest me for putting a match to a twenty-dollar bill when I've already committed the greater crime of making a whole burnt offering of beef for a bunch of turkeys like you? I'll tell you why. Because the beef is mine: real meat, in a real world, with which I can do any real thing I like. But the money is not mine, it's theirs; it's the sacrament of the power of the unreal world, and it must be protected from anyone who even begins to point out its fundamental unreality. The Holy cannot be profaned with impunity."

But to return to the young. Children are first taught that money is valuable in itself. Next, they are taught that it is power: if they have money, they can do things that children without it cannot do. After that, they are taught to value themselves simply because they have it, not because of who they are. And finally, they are taught to value others—and their relationships with others—in terms of the monetary value that can be put on them.

Take, for example, the relatively simple business of giving children allowances. That there are good reasons for the practice is indisputable. Not only is it an act of love, of free grace, on their parents' part; it also enables the children themselves to buy things they can enjoy, or even perhaps give away out of their own love and free grace. But in actual practice, the giving of an allowance is almost always pressed into service as an instruction in the religion of money. Conditions are attached. If children are bad, the money is commonly withheld—a tactic we would probably never even try to justify if we were talking about giving them, say, love, or food, or shelter. If they spend their weekly allotment foolishly, they are lectured about responsibility. And if they simply give it away to their friends, we give them the clearest possible impression that they have come very close indeed to blasphemy. Money must be honored above all; friends should be told to fend for themselves.

In a word, we teach them that everything must be *earned.* And after a very few years of such depressing instruction on our part—and of equally depressing eagerness to receive it on theirs—they become convinced that they *are* only what they're *worth,* not that they are worthy *as they are.* They become committed to a world in which their worth is defined by an unreal set of parameters—by the *works* of the religion of money. Love, given or received, does not define them. Free and gracious gifts do not define them. Nothing that could really and humanly define them is allowed to interfere with the process of definition dictated by the parallel universe. They are, in short, hooked: hooked out of this world and into another.

There is, of course, a cure for the malaise: it is called *giving.* But it is so hard to take that almost no one is ever cured. Christmas presents turn inexorably into swaps. Birthday gifts become rewards. Impromptu largesses carry with them expectations of payback. And finally, the whole business of giving is turned precisely into a business. There must be *good reasons* for giving; recipients must be proved worthy of what they are to be given.

You would think, perhaps, that the Christian church—with its Gospel that *all* religion is now over and done with, and that our relationships with God and each other are based only on gracious gifts—would get this straight. But it seldom does. Look at the average church's pitch for pledges. All it should really say to its members is, "Look, you need to give money away in order to sass the system of money back. Let us have some of what you give away, and we'll get rid of it for you in all the crazy ways we can think of." What it actually says to them, however, is, "We need money to make this shop we've got going look respectable. Here is our budget: study it, and see if you don't think we're a solid investment target." Do you see? The church acts far more often like an institution selling a product to canny buyers than like one offering liberty to slaves of the system. The one outfit that should be the professed enemy of the system is actually, altar, pew, and steeple, in and of the system. The salt has lost its savor.

Giving, therefore—dumb, no-reason-for-it unloading of money—remains the only hope of a cure for the disease of money. As I said, the cure is hard to swallow, and children are no more likely to find it palatable than the rest of us. Even when parents provide good examples of giving, the system of money is still so pervasive that it is entirely possible for their offspring to grow up devoutly greedy anyway. But the example should still be given. At the very least it will provide them with a glimpse of what freedom looks like. Besides, as everyone knows, children have a built-in taste for the profane: here is one place it can be put to good and liberating use.

You have been patient through this long chapter. Let me end it with just a few comments on the religionizing of Love in early childhood.

In spite of my earlier suggestion that we wouldn't attach conditions to love the way we attach them to money, we all too often do just that. Admittedly, our first gifts of love to children are generally unconditional, particularly in the case of those of us who are mothers: bad behavior is not met with threats of withholding the breast. A baby's first lesson is that it is worthy of love—and therefore worthy in itself—no matter what it does. But soon enough, it begins to be taught, and to believe, that it is worthy only if it produces works that can make it worthy—only if it fulfills creedal, cultic, and behavioral requirements. In short, it learns that it must be successfully religious if it is to be of value to its parents. And this religiosity quickly internalizes itself in the growing child. Most of us leave childhood with less of a sense of self-worth than we had when we entered it. If we were not convinced of our unacceptability by our parents before we were five, the school system convinces us very shortly thereafter.

How does this happen? If I had to single out one device by which this religionizing, you-must-make-the-correct-sacrifices-before-you-can-be-loved requirement is laid upon us, I would pick guilt. We learn early that love means *always* having to say you're sorry. From "Mommy is disappointed in you," to "Daddy is angry with you," all the way up to the child-abuser's unappeasable rage, our primary caretakers' primary care seems to be to convince us that it's *our fault* that they are not happy or that we are not loved. Obviously, most parents don't deliberately set out to produce that impression. But their habit of harping on what goes wrong, plus their strange conviction that blaming children is the best way to teach them responsibility, guarantees that the impression is almost universally given.

But blame doesn't lead to responsibility. Responsibility is a positive trait, developed more by acceptance and encouragement than by criticism. Blame is negative; the only thing it encourages is behavior designed to get rid of blame—in other words, behavior that aims not at improving ourselves inwardly but at controlling or appeasing the person who made us feel guilty. But once we reach that state of mind we are chin-deep in religion. We become convinced that acceptance—which is what we most need—is the very thing we cannot have until we have somehow gotten rid of our guilt. Accordingly, our pursuit of happiness becomes little more than a hunt for the right rituals of expiation—a trek, not through the bright and varied realities of this world but through the dark religion-mines of the parallel universe.

Worse yet, those "right" rituals are not easy to find. When we are young, admittedly, our parents prescribe certain simple ones ("eat up your peas, and you'll be Mommy's good little boy again"); but as we grow older we are far more often left to guess at them ourselves. And the older we get, the more onerous that religious guesswork becomes. A four-year-old who has taken his sister's toy has a relatively comprehensible expiation to make: if he gives back the toy and says he's sorry, he is back in his father's favor. But a ten-year-old trying to fathom what to do about her mother's depression is desperately in the dark: by then, she is so used to blame and guilt—and so unused to unconditional acceptance— that she simply assumes her mother's condition is her fault. So she walks on eggs, or avoids stepping on sidewalk cracks, or invokes whatever other religious controls she can think of; but since nothing she does seems to have any effect on either her mother's state or her own guilt, she falls into the ultimate trap of religion: self-loathing and despair.

By the time she is an adult, therefore, she reaches the standard condition of the human race, namely, an utter inability to believe in or even conceive of acceptance as a free gift. Even though her religion has plainly not rendered her acceptable, she is neverthe-less unable to break her addiction to it. And if you then try to sell the notion of grace to such a religion junkie, she will just walk away from you and shop for a fix elsewhere. Any Christian preacher who has seriously tried to convince a congregation that God in Christ no longer has any problems with their sins—that he simply accepts them freely as they are, sins and all, and forgives them out of love— knows that that's the last thing they will ever buy. You can blame them and curse them and threaten them with hell, and they will feel right at home—grateful, as they always have been, for almost any ritual of expiation you lay upon them. But if you preach free grace, every circuit breaker in their heads will pop. You will be lucky if they just look at you as if you were from another planet. It's far more likely that they will make a concerted effort to remove you from this one.

The fact remains, however, that no matter how long or how strenuously we practice our religions of expiation, none of them does the least good. Self-hatred is always at hand, and desperation is just around the corner. And that is because there is no way anyone can *earn* acceptance and forgiveness. If those things come at all, they come as free, unconditional, *unmerited* gifts from someone who has gone out of the blame business and who can thus enable us to get out of the guilt business. They do not come as a result of our works. Forgiveness is never a tit-for-tat response to a sufficient, external stimulus; it is a disproportionate, extravagant laying down of everything—of expectations, hopes, principles, demands, even of life itself—for someone the forgiver has absurdly decided to call a friend. Yet when we train children, that is exactly the impression we do *not* leave them with. Our message to them, loud and clear, is that they cannot be pardoned, unless . . . , that they will be guilty, until . . . , and that the blanks can only be filled in by them. We train them, in short, to rely for their self-worth not on the love of others but on the last thing in the world that can produce it, namely, their own efforts. And in doing so, we teach them to rely on a device that will not only fail them, but will fail them more and more seriously the longer they rely on it. Because the things the "gods" demand as propitiation—the works of religion that our parents, our peers, or any of our other deities lay upon us as conditions of acceptance—increase in difficulty as we advance in age.

Suppose, for example, I have stolen three things from my cousin: her crayons at age four, her virginity at fourteen, and her house, land, and income at forty. If she forgives me any of those depredations, her forgiveness will arise only and freely out of her love; it will never be a necessary consequence of any behavior or promises of mine. Her forgiveness, in other words, lies locked behind a door I cannot even get to. Yet all my training has taught me to assume not only that I can get to that door but that I can, quite on my own, manufacture all the right religious keys to it. The key of kiss-and-make-up, perhaps, for the crayons; the heavier and more dreadful key of promising never to be alone with her again for the virginity; and the key of God knows what inner torment, outward disgrace, and costly restitution for the impoverishment.

Fascinatingly, this lifelong manufacturing of new and more burdensome (but still useless) religious keys is chargeable more to plain old fallen human nature—to original sin—than it is to historic religions. In the first place, as I've said before, the historic religions got their earn-your-own-way attitude from human beings, not vice versa. But in the second, neither Judaism nor Christianity—if you look at their scriptural foundations rather than at the performances of their adherents—give religiousness much houseroom at all. The God of the Old Testament, on any fair balance, desires mercy more than sacrifice. And the God of the New is a downright fool for free grace. Neither Israel nor the church were ever finally told they would have to earn their way to God by their own expiation of guilt; in both cases, God said he would wipe it away all by himself. That Jews and Christians have become obsessed with guilt is not something you can pin on God. We did it to ourselves.

Let me wrap up these preliminary remarks about love and religionizing, therefore, with an illustration from Scripture. Perhaps the best picture of the relationship between them—and of the triumphant breaking of that relationship—is the Book of Job. At the beginning of the story, Job is exactly where we all are as a result of our early and largely disastrous training in love: he is religious to a fare-thee-well. To be sure, he is a prosperous man with seven sons, three daughters, and enough real and personal property to make the Ewing clan in "Dallas" look like welfare cases. But his sense of himself at this point is so dependent on manufacturing religious keys and pulling religious control levers that he runs around offering burnt offerings just in case he's overlooked some essential expiation—even for his children's sins.

But then God himself steps in and begins the long, painful process of weaning Job away from religion. The Sabeans destroy Job's oxen, asses, and servants. A fire from heaven finishes off the sheep and some more servants. The Chaldeans steal all his camels and kill almost all the servants he has left. And a great wind collapses the house in which his children are feasting and kills them all. Job's first response, predictably, is religion: he shaves his head, falls on the ground, and worships—being especially careful not to blame God for the wrong that God has obviously done.

Next, however, God allows Satan to afflict Job himself with loathsome sores from the sole of his foot to the crown of his head. Job's wife adds to it all by giving him no sympathy whatsoever, and his three comforters come and sit with him in uncomforting silence for seven days and seven nights. But then finally, at the beginning of chapter three of the book, the treatment at last begins: Job opens his mouth and curses the day of his birth. He starts the painful process of questioning his religiosity—of recognizing the fact that despite all his efforts at expiation and control, his life has been out of *his* control from day one.

The process goes on for thirty-five chapters. Job insists from start to finish that all human efforts at control are useless. His friends (bolstered toward the end by yet another comforter) keep interrupting him with lectures to the contrary on how he ought to be afraid to say the irreligious things he has been saying. Taken together, therefore, Job's comforters are a perfect example of the persistence and vehemence of the world's efforts to defend religion. Job's irreligiousness is a threat to their whole way of holding their lives together. They argue, they plead; they give him reason after reason and illustration after illustration to convince him that religiosity is the right response. Job, however, dismisses them as cold comfort: despite all their protestations, religion simply hasn't worked.

But then comes the brilliant ending of the book. For the first time, at chapter thirty-eight, God himself appears to Job and delivers a long speech from a whirlwind. Fascinatingly, what he actually says is not all that different from what Job's friends have been saying: God's ways are not man's ways; who is Job to complain? But the fact that it is God in person who finally confronts Job—and that Job is finally able to fall in love with God rather than with religion—is what makes all the difference. As I see it, therefore, the several points of the Book of Job can be tallied up as follows.

1. At the beginning, everybody (Job included) is religious. They are all in love with the system of control and expiation by which they were trained to hold themselves together.

2. As a result of Job's afflictions, he falls out of love with the system of control: he loses his religion.

3. His friends, however, spend thirty-four chapters hanging on to their religion and urging Job to do likewise.

4. Accordingly, when God actually appears on the scene, he does not speak to the comforters but only to Job—that is, to the only person in the book who has finally given up on religion—because Job alone has finally gotten out of the false, parallel universe and into the real one that God himself has made. The comforters, God says, have not spoken of him what is right; but Job, because he has broken with religion, has spoken rightly of God.

5. And to prove it, the last paragraph of the book is a stylized but triumphant vindication of Job: he gets everything back—free for nothing and doubled to boot—just for accepting the real God of the real world rather than conjuring with the gods of the parallel universe.

Do you see? Job starts out in religion, but he ends up in love. To be sure, in the last chapter he understands no more of the

Mystery of Luck by which God runs this world than he did in the first. But he has seen the true God out of whose Bed (if I may revert to my earlier image) the gracious Luck proceeds, and he falls in love with the Home of his being. If Job's comforters were in love with anything, it was their religion, not the God who gave them their being. But Job himself has come full circle to the Love out of which he sprang, so he alone ends up at home.

Getting rid of religion, therefore, is always the first step back to love. Given that, the Love that draws everything home does all the rest.

7

Romance

BY WAY OF A DIVERSION BEFORE TAKING UP YET ANOTHER weighty subject, let me give you a bit of fictitious correspondence I once composed for a friend. Only the names have been changed to protect the guilty.

Arthur Hamish of East Waffle, Rhode Island, writes:

"Reverend and dear Sir,

"I am forty-six years old and I know there are a lot of things wrong with the world today, like inflation, and hypertension, and the threat of nuclear winter, but I had always assumed that falling in love in middle age would somehow be an exception to the downhill slide. I remember an old uncle telling me once (I was about twenty at the time and thought I knew everything about sex, love, et cetera): 'Son,' he said, 'it's not just youth that's wasted on the young. It's romance. They moon their way through it as if it were some kind of church service or patriotic duty. Nosir! Give me two forty-five-year-olds in love any day. More fun than a barrel of monkeys.' I assumed at the time that my uncle was talking from experience, but now I wonder. You see, I recently got myself involved with a lady my own age, and what with the guilt and the indecision (neither of our marriages is all that terrific—in fact, if we're going to be honest, they both had pretty well been deep-sixed years ago, but it's hard to throw the last shovelful of dirt on twenty-five years of your life, isn't it?) . . . Anyway, talk about church services! We go to this county park and make love in the woods and then I find myself getting gloomier and gloomier about how complicated (not to mention expensive) it would be to actually do anything about packing it in with Henrietta. Gloria (that's the lady's name) doesn't have such a big problem with it—in fact, she says she'd walk out of her marriage tomorrow, and I believe her—but I can't seem to make up my mind.

"What I want to know is, is it normal for a man of my age to fall in love and then find it's *less* fun than a barrel of monkeys? Did my uncle lie to me, or was he just talking through his hat?

"Please answer by return mail, as Henrietta has just taken up bird-watching and it's only a matter of time before she discovers the county park system, too—which could drop my fun quotient to something like .003 barrels of monkeys.

Sincerely,
Arthur Hamish"

"Dear Arthur,

"Lucky thing for you that you wrote to an old Thomist dogmatician instead of a psychiatrist or a moral theologian. Those types are always so busy trying to evaluate the history of your traumas or the state of your soul that they never get around to what's really wrong with you, which in your case is that your thinking is a little messed up. What they would take years, or volumes, to sweat through, I can clear up for you with just a couple of good distinctions.

"First, your uncle didn't lie to you; you misunderstood him. Use your head, Arthur! Stop all this quantifying of barrels of monkeys and just think for a minute what the phrase actually means. Since it's unlikely you've ever had any direct experience of the phenomenon, let me give you a little exercise of the imagination to clue you in.

"A barrel of monkeys can hardly be expected to register, in the mind of its possessor, anything higher than the mildest sort of amusement. It in no way qualifies as fun. Think of the problems. Where do you keep the barrel? What do the neighbors do when they find out you have it? And what about all the monkey droppings? How do you get them out of the barrel without being bitten? Can you use them in the garden, or will they burn the hide off your cucumbers?

"But I think you see what I'm getting at. The reason why pleasurable experiences are classified as more fun than a barrel of monkeys is to provide them with a fixed baseline or reference point—a standard so close to no fun at all that it will enable us to measure even the most modest quantities of jollity. Fun—or happiness, to raise the level of the discussion a bit—cannot be expressed in terms of fractions or multiples of barrels of monkeys, or of any other such items that at best can only be considered nuisances to begin with. To attempt such a quantification is to run headlong into manifest absurdity. Consider, for example, the following tabulation:

0.003	bbl. monkeys	=	abject misery
0.82	bbl. monkeys	=	slight dissatisfaction
1.0	bbl. monkeys	=	fun
1.7	bbl. monkeys	=	real fun
2.5	bbl. monkeys	=	sidesplitting fun
3.91	bbl. monkeys	=	totally incapacitating fun

In medieval philosophy, the fallacy underlying this list was named (possibly by St. Thomas himself) "The Aquino Contest Error"—a reference to a medieval joke in which the first prize in a certain contest was one week in Aquino, the second prize two weeks in Aquino, and the third prize three weeks in Aquino. Modern Thomists usually refer to it as "The Philadelphia Misconstruction," but by either name, the intellectual mischief it perpetrates is made abundantly clear. Happiness simply cannot be estimated—and it certainly cannot be increased—by superimposing upon one's life additional barrels of monkeys or extra weeks in either Aquino or Philadelphia.

"Far more important, however, is the corollary to this Thomistic maxim, namely, that happiness is in fact increased only by the resolute elimination from life of any and all barrels of monkeys or fractions thereof. *There,* Arthur—as I think you can now see—is where you have made your biggest mistake. You refer at the end of your letter to the, to you, dire prospect of a 'fun quotient' of .003 bbl. monkeys. (Let me note, in passing, that the only reason I am responding to you instead of writing you off as a hopeless muddlehead is your presumably unwitting invention of the 'fun quotient,' or F.Q. Somewhere, down below the clutter of your thinking, there lurks a laugh waiting to blow every last monkey off the precincts of your mind.)

"In any case, what you must do is clear enough. *All* the monkeys—your guilt, your dread of Henrietta with her Audubon bird tweeter and her sensible shoes, your preoccupation with what is fair to whom, your fear, perhaps, that the neighbors might call in the moral police—must be given the full force of that laugh.

"But note well how you must, and must not, deal with these monkeys. You must not try to prove them despicable, false, irrelevant, or illusory. Your guilt—not only for cheating on your wife with Gloria but for defrauding her in dozens of other ways, no doubt, for the better part of twenty years—is real. You are *not* innocence personified and the sooner you knock off the impossible job of trying to render yourself respectable, the sooner happiness will be able to walk through the presently stuck door of your life. Likewise, your dread of Henrietta must be countered by an eager expectation that she will soon and suitably spot you in the woods for the bare-bottomed mossthrasher you are and begin in earnest the plowing up of your life's landscape that you have so far contemplated only from the comfortable veranda of your mind.

"So too with all your other monkeys of fear or fairness, or of what nature, man, or God might possibly do to make the wheels fall off the little red fire truck of your own good opinion of yourself. Those monkeys, in fact, are not just a single barrel of discrete inconveniences that have kept you so far from anything seriously resembling fun; they are—to say it quite plainly—one and only one monkey, namely, the great baboon of (if I may borrow a phrase from Eliot) 'the endless struggle to think well of yourself.' Eliminate *that* struggle, Arthur, and your F.Q. will go off the scale. Then and only then will you and the (so far as I can tell) admirable Gloria—or possibly, you and the presently unadmired Henrietta— be dealing not with the chimera of respectability you have so long tried to keep perched fastidiously on your back but with the real, if somewhat dung-spattered creatures that you are. Only then will you be able to say to either of them, or they to you, that you are— God help you—all the other has and that, mercifully, you matter more than all barrels of anything. Auden, perhaps, said it best:

> Lay your sleeping head, my love,
> Human on my faithless arm;
> Time and fevers burn away
> Individual beauty from
> Thoughtful children, and the grave
> Proves the child ephemeral:
> But in my arms till break of day
> Let the living creature lie,
> Mortal, guilty, but to me
> The entirely beautiful.

"So there you are, Arthur. We are all s.o.b.s and Jesus died for every last one of us. You've got the ticket to the Supper of the

Lamb in your pocket; for God's sake, get it out, let him punch it forgiven, and get on with the party.

"Good luck to all of you. The enclosed set of high-powered binoculars is a present from me to Henrietta. Call it practical theology. Anything to get rid of that damned monkey.

Sincerely,
Justus E. Peccator"

Lector: Oh, dear me.

Auctor: Ah! Welcome back. Even if you do come with another objection.

Lector: Not with another; with the same one as before.

Auctor: You are referring, I presume, to my reintroduction of adultery into our proceedings.

Lector: I am indeed. Why must you always hoist the Jolly Roger of immorality in front of your readers when—to give you credit for not entirely evident good intentions—you are supposedly coming to them in honesty and with good will?

Auctor: It's a dominical tradition. The Lord himself comes like a thief—and consorts with publicans and sinners in the bargain.

Lector: You are not the Lord.

Auctor: Granted.

Lector: In fact, if I may speak plainly, you sound like little more than an overgrown bad boy who delights in shocking the sensibilities of the upright.

Auctor: Another dominical tradition. Your description of what I sound like fits Jesus to a T. He too delighted in shocking the sensibilities of the upright. Like him, I am simply a devotee of healing on the Sabbath.

Lector: I fail to see how your flaunting of adultery can possibly constitute a cure for anything.

Auctor: Precisely. And you fail to see it for the same reason that the Pharisees failed when Jesus healed on the Sabbath. Like them, you have a deep and abiding conviction that God cannot deal with sin—that sinners have to get their act together before God will condescend to relate to them. But Jesus disagrees. As far as he is concerned, it is precisely sinners who are God's cup of tea. So in order to make it clear that he has absolutely no problems with sinners, he puts himself in a position where the Pharisees will have no choice but to label *him* a sinner, too; he "becomes sin" (to use Paul's paradoxical phrase from 2 Cor. 5:21) by gratuitously breaking the law of the Sabbath in their faces.

Lector: But he, presumably, had higher motives than you.

Auctor: In all honesty, I don't think so. My motives are the same as his, namely, to cure my hearers of their excessive fondness for moralism—to alert them to the alarming fact that (to quote Paul) "while we were *still sinners*, Christ died for us" (Rom. 5:8). The Pharisees, you see, were convinced that religious or moral incorrectness would cut us off from God; but Jesus was persuaded that it was the lost and not the found, the sick and not the whole, the outcasts and not the insiders who are the signs of God's abiding relationship with his creation. Similarly, to come to the difference of opinion between you and me, you are convinced that God runs away from adulterers, while I am persuaded that the Beloved Wisdom who calls the whole world

Home is not one whit less Home calling in adultery than in chastity. I wave adultery in front of you, therefore, for the same reason that Jesus waved Sabbath breaking in front of the Pharisees: to convince you of two errors in your thinking. The first is that you, like the Pharisees, have made cessation of sin into an instrument of salvation. But it isn't, and it can't be. The mere stopping of an adultery, for example, can no more bring you to the Home to which the Wisdom of God calls you than can the stopping of any other sin. For one thing, Jesus says that even *thinking* about adultery is as bad as committing it—and that, if I may be so bold, leaves nearly all of us in the soup. But for another, even if you did manage a lifetime of absolute chastity in thought, word, and deed, you would still be a sinner in some other department—and thus unentitled to throw stones at anybody. Your second error, however, is far more serious. Both you and the Pharisees seem to think that salvation (or, to use my phrase, the job of bringing us Home) is something that cannot happen unless we lend it a helping hand—or at least make a sincere effort at doing so. As I read the New Testament, however (not to mention the Reformers), I get the distinct impression that salvation happens entirely by the free and unmerited gift of God's Home-calling grace and not at all by our works. But this could turn out to be a long digression. Do you really want me to continue mining this totally obvious scriptural vein?

Lector: Yes I do; because I'm still not sure whether you're handing me real ore or just a lot of sand.

Auctor: Very well. Let me give you two illustrations of Jesus' profound commitment to healing on the Sabbath. In the ninth chapter of the Gospel according to John, Jesus sees a man blind from birth. His disciples immediately conclude that such blindness has to be a punishment for sin—either the man's own or his parents'. Jesus, however, says it has nothing to do with anybody's sin; he insists that it is there simply in order that the "works of God"—the way God really works—"might be made manifest" in the blind man. Moreover, he points out that those "works of God" originate entirely and exclusively in himself as the light of the world, and not in the efforts, however upright, of anyone else. So he heals the man then and there on the Sabbath and everybody's mental circuitry goes into overload. The by-standers try to prove that the man whose eyes were opened is not the same person as the blind beggar they had previously known. The Pharisees take the tack that the healing shouldn't or couldn't have happened because God wouldn't grant such a gift to anybody who tried to exercise it on the Sabbath. The healed man, however, sticks to his guns: he says that he's the very same fellow who was born blind, that he knows he was cured by a man named Jesus, and that as far as Jesus' being a sinner is concerned, the whole idea is idiotic—all of which gets him unceremoniously "cast out" by the Pharisees. Now I want you to note something peculiar about that last note in the story so far. Jesus healed the man while he was still a loser: blind, and a beggar to boot. But for all the time of the episode that the man wasn't a loser any more—for all those hours that he was the object of everyone's fascination—Jesus is absent from the story. It's almost as if Jesus is deliberately making the point that he can't deal with someone who's any kind of winner at all. But once he hears that they have cast the man out—that is, that they have made him a loser all over again—then Jesus looks him up a second time and asks him a question that only a loser, apparently, is capable of answering. He says to him, "Do you believe in the Son of man?" (To the formerly blind man, incidentally, this has to sound like a piece of off-the-wall theological chitchat, since up to this point in the story, he has never actually seen Jesus.) In any case, the man simply asks, "Who might that be, Sir, so I can believe in him?"—and that gives Jesus the chance to deliver the punch line he has been holding onto since the beginning of the episode. He says, "You have both seen him, and it is he who is talking to you." And finally the man comes through with the response that only someone who has given up on winning can make: he believes in Jesus (not in a bunch of propositions about moral correctness) and he worships *him* (not his own track record) right there on the spot. Tell me now. Do you begin to see what I'm getting at?

Lector: You're trying to say, I suppose, that Jesus breaks the Sabbath in order to point out that it is he himself, and not anybody's worthiness, or uprightness, or correctness—not even Jesus' own, I guess you would add—that is the only thing that counts?

Auctor: That is very much what I mean. I congratulate you.

Lector: Not so fast. I only said I can see a little better what you mean. I still can't say I'm comfortable with it. Why did Jesus have to make it look so much as if he were *endorsing* Sabbath breaking?

Auctor: Ah! We're finally getting somewhere. You realize, of course, that you have just charged Jesus exactly as you charged me—that is, with the crime of seeming to *endorse* a particular sin just because I use it as an instance of the truth that something far more important than any sin is at work in our midst. Both he and I, you see, are in a bind. If we do not show you that the works of God can take place even in sin, you will promptly conclude that the avoidance of sin is a precondition without which the works of God cannot happen—and that those works, therefore, are not the acts of a sovereign Creator and Redeemer but the ineffective gestures of a God whose hands are tied by sin. In short, you will turn sin into God. Accordingly, both Jesus and I must *seem* to endorse sin in order to keep you from unendorsing God. In fact, though, we endorse neither the sin of Sabbath breaking nor the sin of adultery. It's not as if Jesus

is urging people to break the Sabbath or as if I'm urging them
to commit adultery. Such a notion is simply preposterous. If *good*
deeds can't save people, then *bad* deeds certainly can't save them.
The whole point is that *God* saves people in everything they
do—that the Beloved Wisdom who became incarnate in Jesus
calls them Home in *all* their deeds, good or bad. But since they
are so committed to thinking that only good deeds are acceptable, Jesus and I are constrained to give them bad deeds in order
to unsettle that commitment.

Lector: Well . . . I think I'm beginning to see something, even
though I still don't trust it. Perhaps it would be better if you just
dispensed with the rest of this digression and went straight on.

Auctor: No, no. You said you wanted me to work this vein; I
insist on giving you my other example of healing on the
Sabbath. In the fourteenth chapter of Luke, Jesus does it again,
this time at an afternoon dinner party given by a leading
Pharisee. A man with dropsy is there and Jesus heals him—
right between dinner and dessert, as it were. He prefaces the
healing with a challenge to the don't-break-the-law types who
are present: "Is it permissible to heal on the Sabbath, or not?"
And he follows it up with a flat assertion that when they are
in their right minds, they themselves do very much the same
thing. Naturally enough, this leaves them unable to make any
answer; but Jesus still seems surprised to find them uncon-
vinced by the offensive instruction he has just given. I say
"seems" because he goes right on offending them, rebuking
their fondness for respectability and their dislike for outcasts
and no-goods. He tells them that if they really want to have a
party they should invite the poor, the maimed, the lame, and
the blind—and by extension, any other specimens of broken-
down humanity, sinners included, that they can find. But
then he wraps up all these distasteful illustrations of how God
really works by telling the parable of the Great Dinner Party

(Luke 14:15-24). You can look it up at your leisure; all I want to point out here is that it makes two main points. The first is that the supposedly "right" people (the ones worthy of attending the host's party—the ones, that is, who correspond to the morally upright of this world) were so busy congratulating themselves on their own goodness that they had no time or desire to *enjoy their host's company*. And the second point is that the ones who finally did end up enjoying his company were, to a man and woman, the "wrong" people (the same old list again: the poor, the maimed, the lame, and the blind—the ones, that is, who correspond to all the losers, sinners included, for whom Jesus died). As a whole, therefore, the passage is one more paean to the truth that God has no problem with losers. And it demonstrates the Gospel-rootedness of pushing sinners and lawbreakers at you until you wake up and see that God in Christ has bigger fish to fry than preventing sinners from sinning. His paramount purpose is to drag the whole world into the party; if you make good behavior any condition at all, you blow the Good News of his purpose out of the water.

Lector: Alright, alright. I see your point. But I also think I finally see what my underlying problem has been with it. You say that God's paramount purpose is to drag all sinners into the party. I'll grant you that. I'll even grant that the preachers of the Gospel are under a necessity to "consort with sinners" in their proclamation of the Gospel in order to avoid giving the impression that moral uprightness is a precondition of relationship with God. However—and I hope you will consider this "however" seriously—aren't even sinners, once they have been dragged into the party, under some necessity . . . no, I take that back: it gives you too easy a shot . . . aren't they at least under some *advisability* to stop sinning? Having been found and brought home, shouldn't they try to stop losing themselves—or at the very least, to begin *repenting* of the fact that they are lost?

Auctor: Ah, well done! *Advisability* I will give you. Yes, they *should* try to conform themselves to the style of the party. Yes, they *should* repent. They should put on the free party costume (namely, Jesus' righteousness) that their host has given them. They should not, like the man in the Matthean version of the Great Dinner Party (the King's Son's Wedding: Matt. 22:1-14), leave it in a box at their feet. But for one reason only: *they* will not enjoy the party as long as they fight the costume. But please note this: *only their enjoyment* is up for grabs. Their invitation into the party in the very thick of their unworthiness still stands. Their host's "I want you with me" is still his gracious last word about them. Their sin, even unrepented of, is still no obstacle to his sovereign acceptance of them. Even if they decide to be eternal party poopers, he still wants them: "the gifts and the calling of God are without repentance" (Rom. 11:29). God never changes his gracious mind.

Lector: Why is it that even when you agree with me, I still don't trust you?

Auctor: Probably because the kind of radical grace I'm urging on you is radically outrageous. And possibly because adultery is such an overratedly fascinating sin that it's almost impossible to see the outrage of grace for the sheer fun the adulterers are supposed to be having. In a way, I apologize for using adultery as my bellwether for testing your acceptance of the Homeward call *in all circumstances.* Hardly anyone can resist the temptation to put the arm on adulterers—to urge them to stop enjoying all those surmised pleasures and be miserable like the rest of us. We may cloak our urgings with calls to repentance, but what we really object to is the unfairness of God in letting sinners get away with sin. We are like the elder brother in the parable of the Prodigal Son: any party thrown for sybarites like that is no party we would care to attend. Now that I think of it, I should have waved suicide in front of you instead of adultery.

Lector: Suicide?

Auctor: Yes. It has three advantages when it comes to portraying radical grace. First, it's not nearly as much fun as adultery, so it wouldn't have aroused your envy. Second, it would have eliminated completely the possibility of your urging repentance of those who commit it: if that kind of sober second-thinking is essential to God's operation, suicide is the one place he's simply not going to get it. But third and foremost, since Jesus has taken away *all* the sins of the world (which I believe he has, despite the church's nauseating record of suicide bashing), suicide makes absolutely no difference when it comes to the Homeward Call of the Beloved Wisdom *in all our acts.* Jesus just never stops calling us Home, whether our acts are good or bad, repented of or unrepented of. And if he never stops *that,* then that alone—and not any moral bookkeeping of ours—has to be his last, best word.

Lector: Why didn't you use suicide then?

Auctor: Well, for one thing, because we would never have had the pleasure of this digression. But for another, suicide lies a bit further from the subject of romance (which, if you will recall, is what this chapter is supposed to be about) than does adultery. So on balance I shall stick with adultery. Romance is a fabulous beast: I want you to look hard at what it really is, not approach it as the caged and toothless tiger we have made it with our prescriptions and rules.

Lector: Still, why could you not have begun by displaying it as the preface to a marriage? There are still, after all, perfectly genuine romances that lead to matrimony without passing through the swamp of dalliance.

Auctor: Granted again. But I have every intention of giving you marriage—and sex and love as well—right along with romance. It's just that all those subjects are apples and oranges, geese and swans; I don't want to stew them down into a *confit* before we've had a chance to sort out their individual flavors. So, if you will allow me . . .

. . . let me deal first with your objection to my using an adulterous relationship to introduce the subject of Romance. The plain, historical fact of the matter is that romance as we now subscribe to it—romance, that is, as an earth-shaking, heaven-rending, metaphysically ennobling experience—was introduced to the Western world precisely in connection with adultery. Who were the first great romantic lovers? Were they the dutifully married Guinevere and Arthur, the lawfully joined Isolde and King Mark? No; they were the joyfully loined Lancelot and Guinevere, the star-crossed Tristan and Isolde.

When the Troubadours (who first brewed this high and heady potion) cast about in their minds for that essential equality of man and woman without which romance could never become the Great, Important Subject it now is—without which it would simply have gone on being the inconsiderable, infatuated itch it was for all the centuries before the Troubadours—they rejected like a cold potato the idea of using married lovers. Marriage, as it then was and for a very long time continued to be, was at its best a contract to *achieve* something called love: love was not what brought people to it; it was what they were expected to work at all during the course of it. But at its more common worst, it was a contract to achieve any number of less exalted goals: the joining of landholdings, the cementing of alliances, the perpetuation of the husband's family name—or in the case of the landless, friendless, nameless poor, the provision of one more set of hands to hold the door against the wolves. There was simply too much business in marriage—and too much of that business a matter of male proprietorship—to leave room for the exalted and exalting business the bards of romance had in mind. Arthur might find Guinevere convenient, helpful, kind, thrifty, brave, clean, and reverent—and for all we know, good in bed. But only Lancelot could find her his life, his soul, his self—a self, if you please, he never knew till her.

That was not just heady stuff. It was pure, one-hundred-proof *aqua vitae;* and once the first batch had been mixed, distilled, and marketed by Chrétien de Troyes (12th century A.D.), the world was hooked. For some six hundred years, romance and adultery skipped happily hand in hand while marriage plodded gamely along the rutted ways of parental, if not political, arrangement. But then, in the eighteenth century, we did a remarkable thing. With the invention of the modern novel, we set about the paradoxical task of making romance not the astonishing midnight sun that shone outside marriage but the ordinary, expected dawn of it. Heroes and heroines fell into paroxysms of romantic love and then (because the novelists had carefully contrived to keep them single for three or four hundred pages—you see now, good *Lector,* the historical roots of your preference for marriageable lovers), they slid blithely into conjugality.

But (and this is the second part of my reply to your objection) that was one of the most irresponsible quick turns in the history of Western thought. It was not a smart maneuver. It was not even defensive driving. It was pure recklessness. The point I am about to make is that romance is *always* on the fringes of respectability, *always* iconoclastic. It didn't just begin that way; it remains that way by its very nature. It no more blends smoothly into the routine of marriage now that we have made it matrimony's familiar front door than it did back then when it was a glorious if surreptitious walk around the back yard. Romance, by its very design, is invariably at the hedges of domestic and moral order—if it does not, in fact, break them down completely.

Consider, for one thing, the tradition of the romantic novel. In having its protagonists become romantic lovers and then decide to marry for that reason, it simply swung a wrecker's ball at marriage as the world had known the institution for millennia. Whether that demolition was good or bad (it was probably both)

is not my concern here. My only point is that it was a totally new
and totally final alteration of the human race's mental architecture.
From that momentous late-eighteenth-century day when the first
moonstruck couple decided to defy all parental desires and make
their own marriage on the basis of romance, romance (which hardly
ever needs help at all) has had the whip hand over marriage (which
always needs all the help it can get). Do you see? In its earliest days,
romance was a threat to marriage simply because it was *present:*
whether it proceeded to literal adultery or not, it was always a
blatant infringement upon marital rights. And in our days, romance is still a threat to marriage, but for a new and opposite reason:
now, when we find it *absent* from marriage (as one way or another
we inevitably must), we make it the sovereign reason for getting
out of marriage—because, Lord help us, we claim that its absence
is an infringement upon our personal rights. But in either case, and
by our own deepest convictions, we have spent eight centuries
gleefully appointing romance to be the officer on watch.

True enough, between the so-called sexual revolution (with
its endorsement of casual sex over aeon-spanning protestations of
love) and the discovery by certain advocates of feminism that
romance is just one more subterfuge of male chauvinism, romance
has taken a drubbing. But it is a tough plant and has survived worse
weather than that. The invention of the romantic contraption by
the Troubadours, and the rearrangement of marriage by the eigh-
teenth-century romantic bulldozer, are now in our very synapses.
We can no more go back to the romanceless days before Chrétien
de Troyes, or to the quiet, dutiful marriages before Jane Austen,
than we can to thinking the earth flat or a man's stride the measure
of its distances. All such fantasies are now on the other side of a
great gulf. Any future we have, delightful or dire, will be as
romantic as all get-out.

Anyway (to conclude this rambling response to your indict-
ment), as John Updike pointed out in *A Month of Sundays,* Jesus is
nowhere near as tough on the subject of adultery as he is on
marriage. With the scribes and Pharisees who were chafing at the

bit to stone the woman taken in adultery, he *cranked down* the crime: "C'mon, fellows," he said, "she's just another sinner. If there's anybody here who's not a sinner, let him throw the first stone." And when they all had the good grace to walk off in disgrace, he said to the woman, "No takers, eh? Well then, I don't accuse you either. Go on home and be a good girl." But with the same bunch of upright types who had unuprightly figured out Eight Ways to Divorce Your Wife Without Breaking the Torah, he *cranked up* the requirements of matrimony. "Can't you boys read?" he asked them. "You never saw that 'one flesh' stuff in Genesis? You think your wife is hard to take. Divorce her, and you'll really be in deep trouble."

I don't quite agree with the tack Updike's protagonist takes on these truths. I've come to think that in both cases, Jesus was only trying to convince his critics that they were all sinners and that if they took their stand on the fulfillment of the law, they would miss his whole point—which was that no one stands except by forgiveness. But that's neither here nor there at this point. Adultery may not have changed much since the New Testament, but marriage certainly has. And as for romance . . . well, romance hadn't even been invented back then. So here we are, in another ballgame. Tilt back in your recliner while I try to sort out the names and numbers of all the players.

□   □   □

Let me begin by injecting myself with a little truth-in-advertising serum. I am not now, nor have I ever been, an expert in romance or in anything connected with it. I have had two marriages, quite a few romances, rather a good number (if you're willing to count loosely) of sexual encounters, and a lifetime of aspiring to what I thought I meant by love. But by my own admission—and according to the sometimes vehement criticisms of my assorted or consorted partners—I have rarely distinguished myself in any of those departments.

Of my marriages, one was so short of communication (mostly on my part) that I did it the questionable favor of walking out on it; and the other is such a hurricane of talk (frequently, still, about my self-encapsulation) that I can barely stand, let alone walk. Of my romances, ditto, more or less. They have been good, bad, or indifferent—or (to be honest) glorious, wretched, or mindless: I have racked up my share of miles on all conceivable (and some inconceivable) roads. Of my sexual encounters . . . well, as the tympanist's part usually says during any third movement, *tacet:* don't even *think* of beating that drum. They have ranged from everything to nothing—from the triumphant, full-court press to the ignominious seat on the bench—and both, as often as not, at totally inappropriate times. And as for love? The best I can say is that I still aspire. Even my heaviest breathing, though, remains mostly hot air.

I do, however, have two consolations that keep me very far from despair. The first is that in all likelihood nobody else's track record (yours included, gentle *Lector,* if you are honest) is noticeably better. But the second is that despite the shortfalls of both of us in any or all of these departments, we have never once seriously considered shutting down even a single one of them. Unthinking clergy may bewail the decline of marriage, but with four out of five of the one out of two who divorce heading bravely back for another go at the marital strength test, the statistics are against them. Romance fares just as well: it is still the Great White Queen of our fantasies, even for those of us who may feel we have been banished to the outer marches of the kingdom. Sexuality fares better yet: even though (like Arthur from East Waffle) everyone treats it as if it were some kind of religious observance that no one can possibly get right, nobody doesn't have a sex life, one way or another. Period. And love fares best of all (though it is hands down the worst performed of the lot) for one simple reason: we need it more than air or light: we die without it.

So I do not ask you to trust *me* on these subjects. I ask you to trust *us*—or better said, to trust Whoever or whatever it was that designed us as the marrying, romancing, sexual, loving fools we are. However badly we do these things, they are the sacraments of the greatness of our origin. We may mismanage their liturgies, filling them with high-church flummery and low-church sincerity; we may bury them under blankets of moral earnestness or muffling banks of sentimental flowers; but they still stand as the hallmarks of the *passion/Passion* that creates and restores our greatness. "If I forget thee, O Jerusalem, let my right hand forget her cunning. If I do not remember thee, let my tongue cleave to the roof of my mouth; yea, if I prefer not Jerusalem above my chief joy" (Ps. 137:5-6). These things are the gates and streets of the Beloved City that we are, the precious stones of the twelve foundations of the Bride that the Lamb wills us to be forever. And some day, when we have washed our robes and made them white in his blood . . . some day, thank God, we will finally see what they were all about.

Meanwhile, though, back down here at the ranch—after sixty-five years of hints, guesses, and downright miscues—let me tell you what I think these things have been about so far. Above all, they are about Luck. You have borne with me on this subject before; bear with me a little longer while I press this luck of mine (and yours) further still.

All luck—as I have said, following Charles Williams—is holy. But of all the manifestations of the luck of our being, romance (with its adjuncts: sexuality, marriage, and love) is our principal, ordinary introduction to the holiness that indwells our luck. Take sexuality, for example. It is luck from start to finish. Our gender is not something we have to arrange for or conjure up. It is not even a lucky thing that happens to us. It is, quite simply, *us:* we are male or female from the moment we *are* at all in this world. And it is, at that moment, holy—because the Holy Wisdom wills it in the Bed of the divine Lover.

But that is not all. As we grow gradually over the years (but beginning very early indeed in childhood), this luck of our sexuality metamorphoses itself from dumb holiness—from holiness in mute, unresponded-to fact—to holiness in action, to holiness in power, to holiness with (as holiness must always have) a bark, a bite. There is a story in the sixth chapter of the Second Book of Samuel about a gentleman named Uzzah. The Ark of God—the sacred box containing the two tablets of the Covenant, the box that was called by the name of the Lord of hosts who dwelleth between the cherubims—was being brought back on an ox-cart from its captivity by the Philistines. And David and all the house of Israel played before the Lord on all manner of instruments made of fir wood, even on harps, and on psalteries, and on timbrels, and on cornets, and on cymbals. But in the midst of all this preoccupied virtuosity, Uzzah, noticing that the holy box was about to slide unceremoniously off the cart because the oxen shook it, "put forth his hand to the Ark of God and took hold of it"—and got himself knocked dead on the spot by the holiness of it all. So we, with our sexuality: at six, or sixteen—whenever it is, we are too busy with our own observances to expect it—we reach out to breast or backside, to *pudenda* or *verenda,* and are hit by 220 volts we never even suspected were in the wiring. And from that day on, we are wired for good.

But even that incredible luck, that toothed and fanged holiness, is a mere nip compared to the luck and the holiness of romance. We reach out to it, and are struck dead by it, even earlier than to sexuality. Let me give you an example. When I was somewhere between five and seven years old, I came across a picture in an old novel my parents had lying about the house. It was a line drawing of a dark-haired girl standing on a windy hill. As I recall, there was nothing particularly "sexy" about her: my impression now is that she was quite thin and straight, but maybe her figure was just obscured by the windblown clothes. What caught me, though, was her face. Once again, except for the fact that she had high cheekbones and intense, dark eyes, I can recall it only as a rather lean, conventionally proportioned face. But what I remember about first seeing it is totally out of proportion. Because in that one look I saw and felt something I had never experienced before: homelessness—or more accurately, a dissatisfaction with myself and my surroundings because suddenly everything that mattered had relocated itself into that girl. Which, obviously, was my first decisive if undefined brush with romance—with the diffuse but powerful conviction that I would never again be able to be myself, or to be at home, until I could *find that girl*.

Even then, of course, I knew the usual, sensible objections to such romantic extravagance: it was only a drawing, and only of a girl, and only of a girl in a story at that. But the longing was exquisite and the objections were dull, so the longing outlasted them. And later on, as I looked again and again at the picture (which I did up to some point in my early teens when the novel disappeared from the house), I came up with the even more usual cynical objections: that if I ever did manage to attach such romantic longing to a real girl, it would almost certainly not be reciprocated; that sexuality was in competition with romance and that sexual guilt made me unworthy of it; and that in any case, the fulfillment of that kind of longing would have to wait until I was grown up—whatever that meant.

Still, the intimation of the drawing remained decisive for me, even though I have taken nearly all my life so far to arrive at anything like a definitive notion of what that decisiveness meant. The Victorians loved to specify such experiences as the perception of the perfect "she"—the "her" whom the lover would spend a lifetime looking for in a thousand faces. I think that's over-simplified, if not overblown. Of my own romantic quests, I can only say that some of them did involve women who corresponded to the girl in the picture and some did not; and in both cases, many were muddied or even completely masked by frankly sexual attraction. So as the years went by I pretty much gave up on trying to find the significance of my earliest intimations of romance by projecting them *forward* in any simple sense—by using them, that is, to explain subsequent romances.

To me, now, the only fruitful way to explain them is to read them *backwards*. The girl in the drawing was not an early paradigm of later loves. Rather she was, even when I was only five, a remembrance—or if I may lay upon you another technical theological term—an *anamnesis* of a love that had already called to me and of a home that had already borne me. (*Anamnesis,* by the way, is the Greek word used by the New Testament in recording Jesus' command at the institution of the Eucharist, "Do this *for my remembrance*" [*eis tēn emēn anámnēsin*]. "Remembrance," however, is too weak a translation to convey its force: since orthodox Christians have always held that Jesus is not just mentally remembered in the eucharistic rite but really present in the power of his death and resurrection, the word *anamnesis* conveys the idea of something in the past that is also an ongoing fact in the present. It indicates not merely an intellectual representation of a previous event but an actual *re-presentation*—a *making present once again* of that event.)

Even our first romantic event, therefore, is precisely an *anamnesis*. And I have already said what I think it is an *anamnesis* of: first, it is a making present again of our deep Home in the Bed of the Trinity; second, and more immediately, it is also a representation, a sacramental manifestation, of our earliest home here— of the home into which we were literally and historically born. And all our subsequent romances follow the same rule: they are not the conscious search for someone who matches precisely the paradigm of our earliest romantic experience; rather, they are the constant rediscovery in later loves of yet another *anamnesis* of those same two homes.

And once again, Holy Luck presides over the process: we have our being ultimately by the pure, unfathomable luck of having a God who, in three Persons, unnecessarily wills the *play in Bed* that creates the worlds; and we have our being proximately by all the more recognizable bits of luck by which Mommy and Daddy ended up in their own bed, with whatever genes, gifts, manners, and morals they happened to have. Nobody, maybe not even God, *plans* these things. And even if we say, as we usually do, that God at least *knows* all about them, we certainly can't claim anything like that for ourselves. In all these matters we are in the hands of radically unknowable—and unconjurable—luck. We fall in love not with people whose specifications we have logged into a dating computer, but simply with people we have been lucky enough to run into, given the stringent limitations of time, space, physical energy, and ready cash. We don't know enough about ourselves (or more importantly, about either of the homes that made us what we are) to draw up such a list of specifications; and if we are ever foolish enough to try, we invariably get it wrong. But it doesn't matter, because all of these things—be they sex, romance, marriage, or love—are recognizable in spite of our limitations. Each of them, in its own way, is an *anamnesis* of home. *Thinking* has almost nothing determinative to do with them, and neither does *willing*. They are much more like the sudden transports of the nose's memory—a memory which, at the smell of a perfume or of oily water at low tide, leaps back over forty years and makes whole histories present all over again. In every one of these things, the same lucky, undeliberated transportation occurs: the mind's nose simply *remembers having remembered*—and our clock, for good or ill, is once more decisively wound. "If I forget thee, O Jerusalem . . ."

In fact, of course, none of these things ever quite works out, and some of them work out very badly indeed. But because the *anamnesis* they effect reaches something so close to the roots of our being that it is independent of the occasional sunshine of intellect and volition, their outcomes hardly matter. We are always sitting ducks for the *anamnesis*. We find ourselves quite able—and often ready—to entertain sex after romance, or romance after sex, or marriage after either, or both after marriage. Sensibly enough, we have made rather a lot of rules for ourselves in an effort to put some restraining body English on all this fabulous luck; so much so, that you probably expect me, as a gentleman of the cloth, to say something about the rules. To please you, here it is: *The rules are fine.* But at the risk of displeasing you, I have to say that expounding them is not my cup of tea—nor if it was, would I do it anyway. Because the human race, wisely, has always preferred the fabulous to the sensible, no matter what the cost—not even if the fabulous always made messes and the sensible always made sense. I think, therefore, that we will learn more about ourselves if we refrain from extolling the moral strictures that might (or might not) keep us from breakdowns in the departments of sex, romance, marriage, and love and just look at the subjects themselves, breakdowns included. After all, the triumphs and the disasters alike are both *anamneses* of Home. At best, the rules can only tell you how you ought to maintain the premises of the home you happen to be in at the moment; they can never account for your having loved your way into it in the first place.

One last, corroborative illustration before moving on. At our Church School pageant last Christmas—one featuring a "living crèche" in which the children in the pageant, having taken their places around the manger, held themselves frozen in position while the congregation filed by—I was sitting in the chancel watching the faces of the rest of the children as they stopped to look at the scene. Most of them just looked on with a kind of dutiful blankness—which, as I think of it, was at least an approximation of awe at the Holy. But when my four-year-old grandson was led up by my wife something new happened. His face was blank enough while he looked at the crèche, but as he turned to leave, he spotted a small, blonde girl in a leotard seated on the outer rim of the pulpit. And at that, he stopped dead and did the longest "take" since Laurence Olivier. I've never asked him about it, but I don't have to: his look was unmistakably romance. It was the look of someone who had been stopped dead because finally, in someone he had never seen before, he suddenly saw a home he had known all along but never recognized. Even at four, he remembered something—and that remembrance *re-membered* him: it put him back together as the self he had never recognized but now knew. You may doubt that if you like. But I was there and you weren't. Trust me; whatever I've said about it is less than a hundredth of what happened. It was another first for the fabulous, remembering love.

8

Romance: Further

WHAT ARE WE TO SAY THEN TO THESE THINGS — TO ROMANCE, to sex, to marriage, and above all, to love? I remember a line from Cyril Connolly's *The Unquiet Grave:* ". . . every love-affair must reach a point where it attains to marriage, and is changed, or declines it, and begins to wither." On one level, that is just the lugubriously correct wisdom of a master of world-weariness. Indeed, it comes right after Connolly's withering remark that "Only by avoiding the beginning of things can we escape their ending." Still, I find it cynical to the point of missing the point altogether. That our love affairs inevitably change (and that our sexual relations and our marriages change too, and all too often run downhill in the bargain) is simply part of the "changes and chances of this mortal life"—of the breaks of the Holy Luck that runs the world. Nothing here is immune from the alterations caused by those breaks: not love, not commitment, not life itself. But rather than let the breaks lead me to avoid the beginnings of love, I insist on pursuing it *through* them—all the way back to the ultimate

Beginning that is also its happy End. For even in their worst breaks, our loves do not just break *down;* they break *upwards* as well. And what they break upwards to is Love itself: the Home that invented them in the first place.

But that's too fast and too far to take the subject just yet, so stay with me for a while on the breakdowns. Take the romantic vision. Because romance is a sacrament—an outward sign of the presence of a reality beneath and beyond itself—it is not designed to be the final object of anyone's attention. Or better said, it is designed to frustrate anyone's efforts to pay attention only to *it.* The analogy with the Eucharist here is quite direct. The bread and wine, we believe, are the Body and Blood of Jesus; but precisely because they *are* that, they may be addressed only *as Jesus,* not as some kind of magical bread and wine. So with romance: if you focus on the details of the experience—if you give all your effort to preserving them as they were in their first, gorgeous appearance—you find yourself drifting away from the substance of the experience. And that drift will run you up against one or the other of two very large rocks.

On the one hand, it might run you straight into the hard fact of death. Everything dies; even sacraments, despite the presence in them of their holy substance, remain subject to decomposition. Just as a particular bit of eucharistic bread or wine is not absolved by its sacramental status from the universal laws of change and corruption (even if you wanted to worship it forever, it would sooner or later decay into other elements that are not bread and wine), so every particular romance decays by reason of the natures of the two people involved in it. At the very least, no romance (except as a memory) survives the death of the partners: sooner or later, there are just no bodies—and thus no participants—to keep it going. But even short of literal death, romances pursued as if they were the worshipful reality itself always teeter on the brink of decay. No one in the world is without an ample supply of such things as anger, envy, pride, and sloth. In the first stages of a romance, these things are somewhat held in check by the preoccupying glory of the vision of Home of which the romance is a real presence. But because they have been part of us for a far longer time than the vision—and because our ability to be impressed by the vision is very much a function of its newness in our lives—familiarity breeds its usual proneness to make us act as we have been accustomed to act: to be testy, jealous, self-serving, or indifferent to anything or anybody outside our inveterately preoccupied selves.

On the other hand, the inevitable threat of the breakdown of romance might run you into another rock—a rock I have many times now stigmatized as religion. For just as it would be possible to conjure with the bread and wine of Communion in order to extend their life as sacraments of Jesus (perhaps by laminating the bread between sheets of plastic and carrying it around in your wallet like a credit card, or by keeping the wine in a total vacuum), so it is possible to conjure with the sacrament of romance. People do this all the time. They sense that the signs of the romantic vision (the walks on the beach, the phone calls, the dinners in candlelit restaurants—all the blinding newnesses that once were) are slipping away from them; so they begin the fruitless effort to "put back the romance" in their relationship by putting back the particular details through which they first caught the vision of romance. But it never works. It was the vision that generated the significance of the details, not vice versa—just as it is faith that discloses the bread and wine, not vice versa. And so all their efforts at conjuring—at making a religion of the details of romance—do nothing but saddle them with the old, ineffectual burden of religious observance. The resumption of beach walking, phone calling, or dining by candlelight—the offering of renewed sacrifices to the details of romance—can no more take away the old sins that have returned to bedevil the relationship than could the blood of bulls and goats. Once again, it is the vision that led to the recognition of the details; if the vision is going to be recaptured, it can only be caught by following the laws of the vision, not the laws of the details.

Two things are worth noting before going on. The first is that making a religion out of the details of a sacrament invariably and promptly makes it lose its sacramental significance. The bread of Communion was ordained to be used as bread is used—that is, to be eaten, digested, and evacuated; put it between sheets of laminate and you make it simply unusable: it can function neither as itself nor as a sacrament. Likewise, the events of a romance were ordained to be used as human events are used—to be experienced once and once only and then allowed to proceed beyond themselves into further experiences. Try to repeat them and you get not the original, unrepeatable event but simply a bit of make-believe, of religious conjuring, that gets in the way of (or even precludes) the further, real experiences that are the only things the romantic vision can possibly use as sacraments.

Which brings me to the second thing: the laws of the romantic vision. Because no one can ever go back in time—because, even if nothing else about a particular romance ever broke, there would always be an irremediable break with its past—law number one is that while the romantic experience is invariably a vision, a remembrance, an *anamnesis* of the Home from which we came (and thus can be *understood* only by looking backward and downward), it is just as invariably a vision, a foretaste, a *prolepsis* of the Home to which we go (and thus can be *pursued* only by moving forward and up).

Law number two, therefore, is that far from being daunted by the changes and chances of life—far from fighting shy of the breaks (down, away, out, up) of human experience—the romantic vision is perpetually on the lookout for new breaks *of any kind* in which to re-sacramentalize itself. Romance positions itself in the *next* thing, not in the previous one. As that works out in terms of human frailty, of course, it very often means *in the next romance.* Not necessarily, though. It is entirely possible for there to be a romance of such proportions and commitment that it will never be followed by another. But it is never possible for any romance to work other than by the breaks as they come, not as we attempt to jimmy them back to their original forms by religious conjuring.

Accordingly, the third and last law of the romantic vision is: religion is the death of it. For every romance done in by sin, there have got to be at least five sent down the tubes by trying to conjure up the vision with useless observances. Human cussedness can't hold a candle to the fake, parallel universe of religion when it comes to gumming up any major project. The large evils of the world are not done by mere bad boys; they are the work of highly refined types who are trying to sell another world than this one—and who are willing to sacrifice anything or anybody to accomplish their end. A romance is the beginning of a *relationship;* make a religion of it and you kill the relationship. How many love affairs have shattered, supposedly, on the rocks of betrayal, or jealousy, or putting on weight, or becoming like her mother or his father, when what really did them in was the conviction that the god of romance called for the extermination of the partner rather than patience and forbearance in the relationship?

Sexual infidelity makes a perfect example. A cynic once said that adultery, while it may not necessarily be a reason for divorce in a marriage, always brings about divorce in a love affair. Statistically, I suppose, that's true; but logically, it's a lie. Both marriages and love affairs are relationships; and no relationship in this world can ever survive without forgiveness. Whatever people may *think* about sexual infidelity, it is in fact just one more sin—different in degree, perhaps, but not in kind from any other sin, be it the sin of gross neglect, tyrannical domination, subtle manipulation, or failing to put the cap back on the toothpaste tube. The New Testament never seriously allowed divorce as an option for the so-called innocent party in a marriage beset by adultery; and the church, to her credit, has finally had the grace to stop offering the option—that is, to stop encouraging the religion of marriage that insists that certain sins can only be expiated by ending the marriage. It is time now to bring the same, religion-destroying grace to bear on romance. Even the most outrageous sin against a partner in a relationship is just one more dereliction—just one more of the breaks in which Holy Luck presides over the world. If it is accepted with the forgiving grace by which the Persons of the Trinity exercise their presidency over that Luck, it can always be a break upwards, rather than down.

Which brings us, nicely enough, to the main point. *All* the breaks (exalting or devastating) of *all* our relationships (sexual, romantic, or marital) are meant to be breaks upward into *love*. They are visions, delightful or dire, of the Home that creates us, of the Bed that reconciles us—and because of that they are invitations into the costly, committed, utterly giving relationship of the Lovers—of the Father, and the Wisdom, and the Spirit—from whom we come and to whom we go. Ultimately, of course, that relationship is one of joy: joy at the beginnings of the world and joy in its end. But proximately, that relationship—and all *our* relationships (which are made in the image of it)—are about *passion*. Sex, romance, and marriage are obviously filled with passion in the simple sense of the word: desire and longing are their lifeblood. But just as the passion of the Lovers in the divine Bed led inexorably (given the sin of the world) to the Passion of the Holy Wisdom herself on the cross, so our passions here lead into the Passion—into the love that lays down its life for its friends. True enough, joy is what all passion is about. But in this world it can never come without the Passion—the suffering—into which all passion (innocently or guiltily) leads. Joy is not something we can pursue directly. It is an efflorescence, a by-product of the passion/Passion that is the only thing that can be its occasion.

Hence none of the passionate accouterments of our relation-ships—not the extravagant pleasures of our sexual liaisons, not the till-the-stars-fall, death-and-forever promises of our romances, not the lifelong vows of our marriages—are overstatements. They are merely appropriate responses to the passion that calls us Home. But unless we are willing to accept all the breaks into which that passion may carry us—up to and including the Passion itself—we will welsh on the extravagances and so miss the joy. If the love of the Trinity is not without crisis, pain, and death, ours will not be either.

Thus romance, and sex, and marriage always lead elsewhere, into the Home that beckons us. They are the stages of the journey, not its goal. And so the superimposed "They lived happily every after" I presented you with at the beginning of this book, while it is not altogether an overstatement, still has to be read carefully. If it is taken to mean, "they lived on in the joy of their original romantic event without further effort on their part—without acceptance of new breaks, up or down," it is false. But if it is read as, "they went on accepting all the breaks of Holy Luck and pursued their happiness in each new break either by being open to the newness in gratitude or by reconciling themselves to it through forgiveness," then the statement can still stand. Romance, sex, and marriage, in other words, are not quasi-divine territories—not states with cradle-to-grave welfare programs that automatically take care of the people who happen to land in them. Rather, they are simply ungoverned human states—wild Wests, if you will— in which people have to take care of and with each other. While they are visions, glimpses, even sacraments of home, there are no real *powers that be* in them capable of guaranteeing the sacramental efficacy of any relationship—or even the possibility that it will continue to be a disclosure of the Love that draws us Home. *That* is solely up to us, by the passion, grace, and forgiveness that make all luck holy.

It is never easy. And because it is not, the constant temptation of everyone who points a covered wagon into those territories is to cast about for some way of pretending that there is an administration in them—a government with a beneficent department of welfare which, if we can only find the right numbers to call or the right divine or angelic bureaus to dicker with, will absolve us from the difficult work of learning the bizarre and sometimes dreadful exchanges of the Love that works by sheer luck. That casting about, of course—that hunt for the government that isn't there—carries us straight into the parallel universe of religion; but it also, and at the same time, runs us smack into the untamed intractability of the only universe there is. Let me give you some examples.

Take the sovereign state of sex. Precisely because it is a pleasant place to visit, the benignness of its government is perhaps the easiest to assume: the pleasures of eros having entranced us, we decide there must be laws to enforce their continuance. But when, as always happens one way or another, their discontinuance begins to manifest itself (there are after all only a finite number of orifices and positions, and we have only a limited capacity to remain as entranced by them as we once were), what do we do? Do we accept those changes and try to move with them into the exchanges of Love? We do not. Instead of deciding that it is time to explore our new luck, we conclude that what is needed is some way of conjuring up our old winning streak.

And what do we then do? Well . . . you name it. We consult with gurus who claim to know the laws of the state—who, for a suitable sacrifice of money or effort on our part, will teach us the correct version of the religion the authorities want observed. Or we sit alone and uncounselled and feel guilty about being apostates from the general religion of sex that we assumed to be the law of the land. Or we try group sex, or partner swapping, or one-night stands, or watching X-rated films. And all of it works—but only briefly. We *think,* of course, that it works because we have finally gotten the laws right. In reality, though, it works only for the same reason that anything new works: because familiarity has not yet turned it into just one more same old thing. But when that finally happens, the new religion simply stops working—leaving us a little further along someone else's wagon tracks, but no nearer home. If you can't teach an old dog new tricks, you certainly can't revive an old relationship with them. In fact, you can't go back to the previous conditions of a relationship at all. You have to move *forward* in the ongoing breaks of the relationship—through the deserts, and the flaming arrows, and the bandidos—to the Home that calls you in every event. You have to stop kidding yourself that the parallel universe you've constructed is going to help you find yourself. You have to stop believing it even exists.

By way of another example, take the territory of romance. Once again, its prospects are so fetching that you assume they are guaranteed to stay that way by the constitution of the country. But just as there was no legislature to impose the imagined laws of the state of sex, there is no constitution here either. There are only remarkable experiences, invariably and quickly followed by other remarkable experiences. If you make anything of them, it will be because you learned to commit yourself to the relationship in which they happened and take whatever luck comes your way, not because you found a recipe for controlling the experiences. That, however, is almost the last thing you will choose to do. Because before you will accept the necessity of slogging through the territory, you will try your best to impose the parallel universe of religion on it. Blaming your partner for failing to conform to the religion of the place is perhaps the most common device: "She isn't the girl I first knew"; "He got mean"; "She became a complainer"; "He escaped into his work." But once again, that religion was never real, never *there.* There were no laws, no commandments capable of actually precluding such declines; you invented them. In the real territory of romance, nobody ever declined into someone he or she originally was not. It's just that, in your first enthusiasm for the place, you didn't take in (or others didn't choose to let you see) who and what your partners really were. That they changed in the later stages of the trip is false; the truth is that, with longer acquaintance, you finally learned who they were all along. And at that point, only commitment to each other—commitment to this *him* or that *her,* no matter what overlooked monstrosities we have discovered—can keep the journey Home going.

To put in a kind word for it once again, therapy does help. But when it works, it works chiefly by bringing to light all the unaccepted things in ourselves that have for years been crying out for acceptance—and by placing the forgiveness of our partners' unacceptabilities at the top of our personal list of things to do. It does not work the way a religion promises to work, that is, by giving us conjuring tricks that will make the unacceptability go away. Whether we head west through sex or romance, then, only acceptance—only forgiveness—makes the trip possible.

Marriage, of course, is another country, but it is no more a welfare state than sex or romance. In fact, because it exposes us to all of the unacceptable qualities of our partners and ourselves with a relentlessness those other two states can never match—and because year after year it makes it clearer that what is unacceptable about us is not what we do but *who we are*—the religions we concoct to conjure with marriage are more useless than any others. Making the ritual sacrifice of calling your wife from the office in order to rekindle the fire of your first, romantic phone calls comes a cropper when it dawns on her that you're not going to talk long because you've got a report to finish — and when it dawns on you that she wants to hand you the job of calling the plumber because her biggest worry at the moment is a meeting with your son's guidance counselor.

Nevertheless, rather than admit that the religions don't work—that no such canny sacrifices can take the place of patience, manners, and ultimately, forgiveness—we go right on making sacrifices, up to and including the devastating one of immolating each other in divorce. If I had to assign a single, overarching cause to the high American divorce rate, it would be our refusal to throttle, or even to question, the religion of marriage. Our marital breakups are almost always seen by us—after a few token apologies for our own (pardonable) shortcomings—as due to our partner's unpardonable offenses against the god of matrimony. "He stopped loving me"; "She became a millstone around the neck of my self-fulfillment"; "The magic of the *us* we once had is gone"—all of which is simply additional evidence of our persistent belief in a matrimonial welfare system that doesn't exist, and of our absolute unwillingness to stop making the sacrifices we think the system calls for.

But enough of such depressing unreality. Time to ask the really big question: how, in fact, do good encounters in sex, or romance, or marriage go on into further goodness, as they some-times do? If they are all, to start with, visions of Home and happiness—disclosures in another human being of a life, a self we rush to appropriate for ourselves in the future because we remember and recognize it from the past—how do the successful appropriations work? How, in short, do good encounters manage to avoid the trap of religion and end up flourishing in the real world? I can think of three answers; and at the risk of being a bit cryptic at first, I shall give them to you right now in the tersest possible form before expanding on them at leisure.

The first is the most austere: the sexual, or the romantic, or the marital vision of home, life, and self in another person is gratefully received but then *renounced* as far as any pursuit of it *here* in this world is concerned: each partner's quest for it is directed straight upstairs to God as the ultimate Home. Abelard and Heloise, you will be glad to hear, good *Lector,* will be my illustration of this approach.

The second seems easier but is hardly less difficult: the romantic vision is gratefully received but then *pursued here* in terms of a long love affair (which may even flourish in the thick of the lovers' ongoing marriages to others). Cyril Connolly to the contrary notwithstanding, the King and the Parlormaid will be my example in this case.

The third seems the easiest of all (or at least, the most conventional), but given the witness of the divorce rate, it is no cinch either: the romantic vision is gratefully received, and then *pursued here* in a marriage until death. For illustrations of this one, you and I will have to rack our brains together. On with it then.

Abelard and Heloise took the option of kicking the vision all the way upstairs. They had a verifiable sexual encounter and, presumably, a vision of Home in both that and in the romantic encounter that accompanied it. Sexually, of course, Abelard was forced to punt: he was castrated by the girl's relatives. But romantically, they both had to *decide* on the long kick—which they did, she by retiring to a convent and he by accepting her effective absence from his daily life. They remained in touch to some degree, to be sure: Abelard was marginally involved in the Convent of the Paraclete of which Heloise was abbess. But even that involvement was evidence of the way they sent the vision they found in their relationship *straight Home:* witness the great medieval hymn, *O*

Quanta Qualia, that Abelard wrote for Saturday vespers at the convent. It is a prime example of romance transported all the way forward to the Bed that first called it into being. I give you the fourth stanza, first in English, then in Latin.

> Now, in the meanwhile, with hearts raised on high,
> We for that country must yearn and must sigh,
> Seeking Jerusalem, dear native land,
> Through our long exile on Babylon's strand.
>
> *Nostrum est interim mentem erigere*
> *Et totis patriam votis appetere,*
> *Et ad Jerusalem a Babylonia*
> *Post longa regredi tandem exsilia.*

I want you to notice two things about those lines. First, they are plainly about the *patria,* the *Country* of which the territory of romance is a sacrament. The whole hymn, in fact, is about "Jerusalem" as the Home this world sprang from and thrusts toward. But second, they are not at all about religion. They are not an attempt, in some pious code, to conjure up again the circumstances of the romance that Abelard and Heloise once knew. Rather they are a direct transposition of that romance to the God, and to the New Creation, that made their romance what it was to begin with. They do not try to ace out the exile, the *exsilia,* the Babylon that all human beings, no matter how they answer the vision of home, experience. Instead, they accept both the vision *and* the exile and head resolutely for the ultimate Bed of the divine Lovers—of which the vision and the exile as well are sacraments.

To see how that is *not* an act of religion, consider once again a parallel with the sacrament of the Body of Christ, the bread of Communion. What would you do if you were on a desert island and had nothing that in any way could be considered bread? The *religious* answer would be: celebrate the Eucharist with something else you could conjure yourself into *pretending* was bread—a mango, perhaps, or a banana. But that's the wrong answer, because the bread is just the promised sacrament of Jesus, not the ultimate place of Jesus. Lacking bread, what you should go to is not bananas, but the ultimate place of Jesus himself—which, as far as this world is concerned, is at the root of the being of every single thing, yourself included. In short, you should go directly to Jesus himself: you should *pray;* you shouldn't bother with trying to fake out a Eucharist.

So with Abelard and Heloise: their first sacrament of home (their romance) having been rendered unavailable to them by circumstance and choice, they did not invent a religion of romance to conjure up some quasi-sacrament. They did not (we presume) spend hours writing unsent love letters or putting fresh flowers every day in front of each other's portraits. Instead, they betook themselves—*without religious conjuring*—directly to the pursuit of the Home of which their romance was a sacrament: they applied themselves not to each other (much less to religious imitations of each other or to a faked-out version of the country or romance) but to their ultimate Home: the Land of the Trinity that was their beginning and their end.

As I said, such a radical transposition of the romantic event is not for most of us—not because it is necessarily harder in the long run (it may in some ways actually be easier) but because the world *here* is, rightly or wrongly, more vivid to us than our Home *there.* So we opt instead for pursuing the vision *within* the circumstances of daily life—which works out, given the matters we are talking about, either to a long love affair or to marriage. Take the option of the love affair first. The King and the Parlormaid (or any couples who attempt to bring off such a pursuit) will need a great deal more than the enthusiasm of their first romantic encounter. Besides the general political savvy required to avoid being found out, they will require a profound openness to learning the exchanges of love as the breaks of life present them. They will need patience and forbearance with the circumstances of their romance. *Unavailability* must be borne cheerfully and without blaming each other for it—and it must never once be faked. The *love due to the others who remain irrevocably in their lives* (the Queen leaps instantly to mind) must be genuine and forthcoming. And their *commitment* to each other will have to weather all the storms that such commitment inevitably experiences: the daunting discovery of all the shortcomings that either of them brings to the relationship; the teeming brood of potential disappointments that familiarity begets; the unenchanting ravages of growing older; and sooner or later, the emphatic period, the full stop, that death will inevitably put to their affair.

But above all, they will have to avoid (every bit as much as Abelard and Heloise) even the least flirtation with making a religion of their affair. They must pursue it in the real world—on the wild frontier where no luck can ever be conjured with and nobody can recapture the past. They must avoid like the plague the parallel universe where the success of such stunts is glibly promised but never delivered. And more than anything else, they must accept gracefully and forgivingly the home truth that no home here can be Home—that every vision we catch of Home is a sacrament against the day when sacraments will cease and we will finally see ourselves Home for good and whole for the first time. *That* is what it is all about. That final *turn-on* is why we were turned on here at all. We have always been called *forward;* it is only religion that pretends there is a way of going back.

We are left at the end, therefore, with marriage, which, despite its popularity, is not one whit less demanding a pursuit than the one chosen by Abelard and Heloise or the King and the Parlormaid. Everything I have said about the rules of their pursuit applies here: it must take place resolutely and in the real world, not in the make-believe universe of religion; it will require the staunchest acceptance of all luck (no matter how inconvenient or disappointing) as holy; and it will call for an absolute renunciation of conjuring. But there is this to be said for marriage: even though married couples try just as often as any to lay upon themselves and each other the useless exercises of religion, there is no place more than in marriage where they so emphatically do not work. Nowhere does familiarity breed all its nasty children more than there. Nowhere does the need for grace and forgiveness more regularly arise. Nowhere are we so uninterruptedly presented with the bitterness of the real rather than the nutrasweetness of pretense. And nowhere is *who we are* so painfully evident and *what we say* so manifestly irrelevant. If there is a single lucky break that matrimony bestows on us, it is the breakdown of all our attempts to conjure with it—its insistence on dragging us forward (kicking and screaming, or smiling and pardoning) into the new realities that alone can be new sacraments of Home.

Sex, romance, and marriage, then; these three. Like everything else in the world, they are *anamneses* (remembrances) and *prolepses* (anticipations) of the Home from which we come and to which we go. But preeminently—because, more than most things, they are visions *through another,* gifts *from another*—they are the grand sacraments of the fact that Home is in the end a *relationship.* We are not artifacts destined for an eternal mantelpiece; we are the beloved called by the Beloved herself, the incarnate Wisdom of the Father, into the last relationship of all: into the joy of the divine Lovers in the Bed of their eternal affair—into the exchanges of the Godhead itself—into the Love of the Father and the Son in the unity of the Holy Spirit.

That, at last, is what we were always up to. That, finally, is Home.

9

Vocation

AS WE WORK OUR WAY TOWARD THE END OF THIS BOOK, THE next matter that presents itself is, fittingly enough, *work* itself: not only the various jobs we find ourselves occupying in the process of making a living but also the other careers, tasks, and even hobbies that a world run by Holy Luck drops in our laps. As you can see by the title of this chapter, I am going to lump them all under the heading of *vocation*. But I need to give you a preliminary warning: I am not fond of the usual distinction between vocation and avocation, between work and play. To me, work that does not rise to the level of play is flawed work and play that is simply an escape from the expenditure of effort is flawed play. And I have already given you the reason for that opinion: if we are made in the image of God, and if God's supreme reason for making anything is the divine play of the Father and his Beloved Wisdom in the Bed of their love, then play is the sovereign category, not work. If we have any final vocation, any ultimate calling, it is into that play. All the particular sacraments of that calling, therefore—positions we hold in the world of business, states of life like parenting that often call for harder work than any job, or even the dedicated fooling around we lavish on gardening, or woodworking, or music—all these are conceived wrong if they are not followed as so many calls into the play that is our final Home.

But because that's far too fast a shuffle for so specific a subject—because vocations always present themselves in singular ways to unique persons—I propose to speak here only of the vocations I know something about, namely, my own. I cannot promise you that I will avoid abstraction altogether, but I can at least commit myself to being as anecdotal as possible. That way, any flights of fancy that occur will be entirely my own, not guesses at somebody else's. For the record, I shall be talking about just two vocations: my call to the priesthood, and my call to writing.

First, though, let me bring the meaning of the word *call* down from the sky in which it is usually parked. None of my vocations involved voices from heaven, or even voices inside my head. Instead, they were the result of perfectly ordinary—and therefore holy—luck. They *befell* me: they happened gradually and then went on happening because I said yes to them—or more accurately, because I said a series of yesses to a series of happenings. I don't rule out the possibility of voices from heaven, of course. If God chooses to call Saul of Tarsus or Elmer of Akron by that method, he's free to do so. But I have two thoughts about such calls. The first is that for all their supernatural trappings, they have to be dealt with simply as additional happenings in a world already full of happenings: they acquire their full-blown status as vocations only when Saul or Elmer, in some down-to-earth way, says yes to them. And the second is that I think they are rare: on the available evidence (even in Scripture), God seems to prefer the ordinary leading of luck to the miraculous intervention of loud noises. God does issue the occasional dramatic call; but the still, small voice—and his patient wait for our answer to it—remains his way with most of us.

For openers, then, my vocation to the priesthood. I recall

three stages in my journey to it. The first was the discovery—amidst the carpenter gothic charms of my home parish (I am a lifelong Episcopalian)—that under the familiar, low-church smell of furniture polish and musty red velvet kneeling cushions, there was the incense of the Catholic faith. This happened sometime during my later years in high school when I was given (I forget by whom) a devotional manual called *The Practice of Religion*—an Anglo-Catholic document that introduced me to features of Anglicanism (like fasting on Fridays, and ashes on Ash Wednesday, and going to confession, and preparation for Communion) that to many Episcopalians were simply importations from Rome but to me were visions of Home. Suddenly, I remembered something I had never been taught but recognized as soon as I saw it—and the *anamnesis* caught me where I lived.

Next came the accidental (read, lucky) discovery, only a little later on, of another book. All through high school I had been preparing for a career in naval architecture: the assumption was that I would take the entrance examinations to Webb Institute in the Bronx (which was then a one-hundred-percent scholarship school that guaranteed placement in the profession) and thereafter be set in a career for life. But in my senior year, while browsing in the religion section of my local public library, I came across Harry Emerson Fosdick's *The Light of the World*—and the vague notion of someday, somehow, doing something about the ministry first occurred to me. At the time, I did nothing about it: I read the book once and returned it. To this day, I cannot tell you what it was in the book that struck me. In fact, I have never even looked at it again.

But then luck intervened once more. Because America was at war in my senior year, and because Webb Institute had been taken over by the Navy as part of the V-12 program—and because my eyesight was terrible—I got no closer to Webb than the eye exam in the Navy physical. I read three lines on the chart, was disbarred from taking the entrance examinations, and went to Columbia College instead to study mechanical engineering. I began there in July of 1943 (it was wartime: schools ran nonstop) and in August of that year, I drifted, for reasons as unclear to me now as they were then, into the office of the Chaplain of the University, Stephen Bayne. For the first time (probably because I had quickly found mechanical engineering to be not my cup of tea) I mentioned the possibility of the ministry to someone. After a half hour or so of listening, the Chaplain asked me what I was waiting for. Since I didn't know the answer (that was the first time I had even entertained the idea that I *was* waiting), Stephen Bayne picked up the phone, called my advisor to switch me from engineering to liberal arts, and then called the Rector of my home parish and told him to make an appointment for me to see the Bishop of Long Island.

I kept the appointment, attended a quiet day held the next week by the Bishop for his candidates for the ministry, learned more in that one day about the priesthood than even *The Practice of Religion* had suggested, and just said yes. I was seventeen. In many ways, it was the last vocational decision I ever made: I have been a priest for forty years.

At first, I conceived of my vocation as a call to a peculiar state—to something that other people did not and could not share in. But that was back in the not so good old days when we were taught (and believed) such things. Since then, I have come to a better, more sacramental understanding of both the priesthood and my vocation to it. Priests, as I see them now, are not the possessors of powers that other Christians do not have (*all* Christians are fully possessed of the priesthood of Jesus); rather, the ordained priesthood is a sacrament, a real presence of Jesus' priesthood, held up before the church as a mirror in which others can see themselves as the priests they already are. And the *vocation* to the priesthood, despite the high-flown language in which it is sometimes couched, is not a call more noble than God's other calls to plumbers, computer operators, doctors, lawyers, and Indian chiefs; rather, it too is a sacrament, a mirror held up to the world to remind others that they, every last one of them, are likewise called by God. It's not that the notion of vocation belongs only to the priesthood and is loaned out to lesser breeds to clothe them with a dignity they don't really possess; it's just that every step of everyone's life—from birth, to sexuality, to romance, to marriage, to parenting, to work, to aging, to death—is more a response to the call of another than it is an instance of self-starting. The priesthood is simply a banner of that call that God has run up over all people.

There is one other thing, though, that I have learned about vocation from my life in the priesthood. Every call from God, whether into some dull line of paid work or into an excursion from such work, is a call into play—into *fun,* if you will. If you turn it into mere labor, or into a career, or into a way of making money, it will either blow up in your face or burn you out—or both. To help you see what I'm getting at, let me give you in a few paragraphs some of the things I think I can honestly say about the time I have spent in the priesthood.

1. I have never done an honest day's work as a clergyman. In fact, I hate, despise, and avoid at least half the things clergypersons are supposed to do. I love preaching, celebrating the Eucharist, teaching, and counselling; so I have done those things just for the joy of it. I am also moderately fond of administration (which I delight in doing as quickly as possible), and I am more than a little enamored of ecclesiastical politics (which I have pursued with relish, if not always with success). But I have little love for writing newsletters, attending other people's meetings, paying house calls, or visiting in the hospital; so (since they are no fun), I have done as little of them as I could get away with.

2. Therefore, while I have all my days thought of myself as a priest, I have never thought of myself as having a career in the church, or even as working for the church. To people at Saturday night parties who say to me, "Well, I guess tomorrow is your busy day," I always say, "No, tomorrow is my day off: it's no work at all, just a lark." As far as I'm concerned, I

have had forty years of a *vacation* to the priesthood. I have been paid (on and off, and anywhere from poorly to tolerably—though rarely well); but I have never counted a cent of it as the due reward of any labors on my part. In my mind, the whole clerical "profession" is a splendidly corrupt business that pays me simply for being what I want to be: a priest doing the priestly things he loves.

3. Admittedly, not everyone in the church sees things my way. But that's their loss, not mine. While others were trying to torture me into burnout with despicable buzzwords like "accountability," I have remained comfortably cool. My advice to anyone contemplating any ecclesiastical activity is, "If you can't figure out a way of doing it for fun, do yourself and everybody else a favor and don't do it."

Accordingly, I really do see the priesthood as a sacrament, a grand paradigm of what I think everyone ought to be doing with his or her vocation, namely, to be bringing it as soon as possible and as close as possible to an *avocation*—in the best sense of that carelessly used word. In order to get at that best sense, though, we have to wade through some unfortunate meanings that have become attached to it. The word, by its Latin roots, means a *call away from* something. But in its common acceptation, the "something" that people think their avocation calls them away from is their vocation itself—their underlying conviction being that vocation is by nature all drudgery and avocation nothing but fun and games. But that's as wrong as it is mischievous. Both vocation and avocation are mixtures of drudgery and fun. In spite of what I said about larking my way through the priesthood, it still involves (even for a maverick like myself) a fair amount of inescapable dog-work. And in spite of what I might tell you about the pleasures of my avocation of woodworking, for example, it too involves a good bit of painstaking time at the workbench. But whether we are talking about vocation or avocation, fun must always remain the sovereign consideration. For while it is a truism that nothing that is fun can be done without some measure of discipline, it is practically an eternal truth that nothing that calls for discipline will be kept at very long (or very well) if it is not fun.

So as I see the two words, they are the obverse and reverse of the single coin of vocation-avocation—of the coin of God's lifelong *call* into the play that is our Home. But the very nature of that call—whether vocational or avocational—is that it is inevitably an invitation *from* something *to* something—from *where we are* to the next step *away from where we are*. And therefore every vocation must necessarily be an avocation, and vice versa—a call away from the point at which we have arrived in our calling to something forward of that point to which we are sacramentally invited by the same calling. Specifically (to put it in the terms of this book), vocation-avocation is always a sacrament of the call from the home we are presently in to that happiest Home that is our beginning and our end. Accordingly, it is precisely the people who see that clearly and act on it resolutely who are happier in their several callings than most. They even seem to live longer.

Take concert musicians. Take symphony conductors in particular. Their vocation—the work for which they are paid—is about as close to play as you can get. And if they have the good sense never to forget that, never to do their jobs primarily for any other reason, they have great staying power. Or, to return to the vocation I have been at the longest, take priests. The ones whose primary view of their calling is something other than the fun of the priesthood—who see it as a road to success, or position, or power, or reputation (the definitions of which are entirely in the hands of other people)—either burn out early or shrivel gloomily in harness. But the ones who refuse such alien definitions and do only the priestly things they love doing remain remarkably green and pleasant, both in themselves and to others. Their vocation-avocation is always a response to the call forward toward Home, never a preoccupation with distractions from that call. And because of that—because they are on the move to a happy place, not stuck in a job that is going nowhere or that has arrived at just another job—

they are, quite simply, a lot more cheerful than most of their brother and sister priests.

But enough about the priesthood; time now for some illustrations from the other of the two vocations I promised to talk about, that of writing. Once again, it was luck, not visions or voices, that was the principal device involved in the issuance of the call. For one thing, I had the genetic luck of being born with a liking for words and a certain knack of putting them together. For another, the years of my schooling (the 1930s and '40s) were fortunate. I cannot claim, of course, that my education was as good as that received by some in earlier generations and centuries. T. S. Eliot's lines always haunt me:

> . . . And what there is to conquer,
> By strength and submission, has already been
>   discovered
> Once or twice, or several times, by men whom
>   one cannot hope
> To emulate. . . .

Still, my schooling was a good deal better than what is generally available now. For yet another bit of luck, I happened to fall in love with certain first-class writers (notably John Donne) whom I adopted the conceit of imitating. And for a final set of happenstances, when I did actually write my first book, I also happened at the time to have a student, who happened to know an editor at *Fortune,* who happened to have a friend at Simon & Schuster, who happened to like the book when she read it—and who just happened to get it published.

And seventeen or so books later, my calling as a writer still goes forward by luck. I have had two books that were best-sellers (and therefore fifteen that were not), thus making me what is called a mid-list author: one whom publishers are still willing to gamble on, but only for exceedingly modest stakes. I have also been in and out of the business of writing food pieces for magazines and newspapers: in, because editors liked my work; and out, because those same editors moved on to other things. (You learn one thing as a professional writer: you may think you have a dependable relationship with, say, the *Times* or *Redbook;* but when your editor leaves, the relationship disappears. At a party once, I bewailed this home truth to a man in the pants business. He said, "Tell me about it. I used to think I sold Macy's; but when my buyer left, I wasn't selling Macy's anymore.")

Nevertheless, I still write. And I write for the same reason I am still a priest. It is my vocation-avocation: I do it for fun, not fame or fortune. And that again is luck, because of all the things you can't possibly do for any predictable return in money or reputation, writing has got to be right up there in the top ten. One of my all-time favorite pieces of work was never published as the book I intended it to be: it came out as two separate books, one drastically cut and the other completely rewritten. And another book—the one that, hands down, was the most fun for me to write—accumulated a total of twenty-five rejections before a publisher brave (or foolish) enough finally accepted it. (He was, however, more than careful enough: there was no cash advance in the contract.)

Do you see? If writing wasn't fun, I wouldn't be doing it. Not for one year out of my twenty-five as a money-earning writer did I ever make a living out of it. If I were in it for the money, I would have gotten out of it long ago. But I didn't. And not because writing is such unadulterated fun that every day I find myself chafing at the bit to head for my desk and romp my way through page after page of deathless prose. As I said, every vocation-avocation has its share of drudgery, and writing is no exception. There are, of course, days and even weeks when it goes well. But there are more that don't: blank pages or blank computer screens are very blank indeed. Beginning a book can be hell; and writing a proposal for a book (writing about what you are *going to* write—which is not writing at all, but pure hot air) is the bottomless pit. So if it wasn't in some profound sense fun—if all the discipline of writing wasn't accepted by me as the necessary condition of my catching the vision of Home, of my becoming who I am called to be—my vocation as a writer would just have gone *pffft!* into the general burnout that comes when any vocation is followed for reasons other than the joy of the vocation itself.

Which brings us back to my favorite bugaboo, religion. Pursuing a vocation without at the same time accepting it as an avocation—pursuing it, that is, as a call into *some other thing outside the vocation* rather than as a call *forward into the next thing that the vocation itself presents*—is a fatal fall into the parallel universe of religion. Because once you put all your energy into responding to such calls into other things—into pursuing your career as a clergyman, for example, by making the sacrifices necessary to advance yourself in the church; or into furthering yourself as an author by letting money dictate what, or even whether, you write—you simply make the other things gods and indulge yourself in the hope that they, when properly propitiated, will condescend to govern your life benignly.

In fact, though, the territory of vocation (like the states of sex, romance, and marriage) has no such government. It has only the frontier anarchy of its own nature. If you are willing to go with the luck of that anarchy—if you are willing to put up, say, with anything priestly (good or bad) that comes along next, or anything writerly (wonderful or dreadful) that befalls you tomorrow—and either accept it with thanks or reconcile yourself to it by forgiveness, then your vocation can stand. But if you insist on waiting for your nonexistent gods to intervene and make your vocation all niceness and no nastiness, then the wait will wear you out. And the reason for that is simple: the parallel universe in which your gods have their beneficent powers of arrangement has no connection with the real world in which the true God is content to let things arrange themselves mostly by luck.

As a matter of fact, the only thing the parallel universe is good for is a joke. It was invented to explain how you can put a pair of socks in the dryer and find only a single sock at the end of the cycle. The inhabitants of the parallel universe, so the joke goes, are all one-footed aesthetes: assuming that we are just like themselves, they feel free to relieve us of something as unnecessary as a second, boringly matching sock. But since they also have consciences, they feel obliged to send us something in return. So what do they do? They send wire coat hangers. And that, Virginia, is why you can insure on Monday that your hall closet contains nothing but wooden hangers—and on Friday find it half full of wire ones again.

Such frivolities aside, though, when we seriously and religiously expect the parallel universe to help us with our vocation, the joke (and it is a bad one) is on us. The only thing you can do with your calling is go forward in it *on the terms of whatever luck it may bring.* You cannot conjure with its past in an effort to revive its previous conditions. Consider Smith, who was about to be fired. He protested to his boss that his dismissal was unfair: after all, he had given the firm the benefit of twenty years' experience. "No," said the boss. "Your problem, Smith, is that you have fobbed off on us one year's experience twenty times." So to attempt to go *backwards*—to try, for example, to write a book that will repeat the success of an earlier one, or to rework old ideas that happened to sell well at the time—is to abandon the vocation of writing for the religion of money, fame, or previous pleasure. The real world, more often than not, punishes sequels. Almost no one can write a good one. As Eliot said in the same passage I have already quoted from:

> . . . one has only learnt to get the better of words
> For the thing one no longer has to say, or the way
> in which
> One is no longer disposed to say it. And so each
> venture
> Is a new beginning, a raid on the inarticulate. . . .

And to attempt to go *forward* on any terms other than the vocation's own is just as impossible. There is no supreme court in the country of your calling that will declare unconstitutional the world's failure to bestow on you rewards proportionate to your labors or your worth. That tribunal exists only in the parallel universe; and no matter how much of your energy and resources you spend on lawyers to represent you before it, it has no power at all in the real world. The only vocational reward guaranteed by reality is the reward of the work itself—the fun of either doing the job gratefully or laughing at its disappointments forgivingly. Beyond that, there simply is no other justice here.

But if you insist nonetheless on pursuing vocational justice—if you cannot let go of the idea that the parallel universe *should* be able to intercede for you—you will drown in one or the other of the two inevitable results of such religiosity: worry or bitterness. Take worry first: the terror by night, the famous 3:00 A.M. monster. Why do you lie open-eyed in the dark fretting about all the terrible things that might happen to you in your vocation—in a panic over what more you might possibly do to keep the wolf from the door or the boss from your throat, in dread of what you have left undone and of what is now and forever undoable? Why, in short, are you so afraid of what will happen? I shall tell you why. Worry is the reverse of a coin whose other side is control. Commonly, of course, you think it's the front side and spend all your time preoccupied by it. But if you turn it over and recognize its true nature as a by-product of the effort to control your life rather than accept it as it happens—and then ask yourself where you ever got the notion that you were actually in control of all these terrors that are in fact beyond your control—you will quickly learn the answer. You got that illusion from the parallel universe. You got it from believing in a make-believe world full of *shoulds* and *oughts,* full of imagined courts that have denied your appeal because you filed the wrong brief or replete with imagined welfare bureaucracies that might have helped you, but whose addresses you could never find. You got it, in other words, from thinking that happiness could be secured by religion.

We are back yet again at the connection between *happiness* and *happening.* We are face-to-face with the hard fact that the real world is in charge only of the happenings—and in charge of them almost entirely by luck. You alone, therefore, are in charge of your happiness: if you decide to accept the world's luck by grace and/or forgiveness, you will be happy; if you try to conjure with that luck, you won't be—because the religion of conjuring never works, it just gives you all the worries that can be produced by the false expectation of control. And the fascinating thing about those worries is that, unlike real troubles, they arrive all at once, with each one insisting (successfully) that it be accorded the full measure of dread that the whole lot of them inspires. Troubles can't do that. If at midnight your trouble is that your teenage son has defied you for the nineteenth time and stayed out past his curfew, that trouble will vanish at 3:00 A.M. when you learn he is paralyzed from the waist down as a result of an automobile accident. Troubles come single file, with the biggest bully always preempting the lead; worries come spread out east to west across the whole horizon: even the ones that can't shoot straight scare you to death.

If, therefore, you could manage to pay attention to your troubles instead of your worries—if you could decide to accept the real world whose happenings come to you one by one rather than the imaginary world whose terrors are under no such limitation— you might, by accepting those happenings, get a leg up on happiness. But alas, most of us are far too much true believers in the religions of the parallel universe to do such a relatively simple thing. Take, for example, something that is a stock-in-trade of the six o'clock news: the murdered policeman's widow who is being interviewed on the occasion of the commutation of the murderer's death sentence to life without parole.

Reporter: How do you feel about this?

Widow: (Sobs)

Reporter: Do you think the governor should have let the death penalty stand?

Widow: Yes.

Reporter: Why?

Widow: He took my husband's life; he should pay for that with his own.

Reporter: And so you are unhappy?

Widow: Yes, very.

Do you see? Rather than face the real-world trouble of accepting the husband's death, both the reporter and the widow are involved in a conspiracy to blame her unhappiness on the failure of this universe to live up to the rules of the parallel one in which they have chosen to believe. But those rules, no matter how many people give them credence, can do absolutely nothing to make anyone happy here. In the real world, there are only two things that could possibly contribute to the widow's happiness. One is the return of her husband to life, which is not likely; the other is her acceptance of his death, which she might possibly take a crack at. But for her to make a human sacrifice of someone she hardly knows, in order to even a score the actual universe is not keeping, is monumentally irrelevant. It would also be ridiculous—except that it never makes anyone laugh.

Instead, it makes them bitter—as do all such ineffective sacrifices to nonexistent gods. "This shouldn't have happened to me" is not a happy epitaph; the stroller in the cemetery will always have the apt, last word on it: "Tough luck, Harry; it did." And any life lived under such an unaccepting inscription—or, to the point, any vocation pursued under it—will not be a happy one either. Because while tough luck never totally spares anyone, it is just as holy as any other kind of luck. So if our happiness comes from the Home that calls us in all luck, we had best get on with the acceptance of whatever breaks our vocations hand us. If our luck is not all beer and skittles, it is still the only authentic sacrament of our call—the only place where, while the world lasts, the Holy Wisdom that made us for the fun of it ever promised infallibly to show up.

On the cross, Jesus comes into the world's toughest luck. And he comes into it to *raise the dead,* not to reward the deserving or promote the successful—or to do anything even remotely like the scorekeeping that the myth of the parallel universe insists on. He comes not to jimmy our luck but to take us Home in it. Work at your calling, therefore, and forget about anything else. Do the next thing and let go of everything else. The next step, whether it's up to the top or over the cliff, is the only safe one.

Go nowhere but there and you'll always be Home.

10

Well-Being

FOR THE LAST THREE CHAPTERS, WE HAVE BEEN DRIFTING casually through the main subjects of this book—but in reverse order. Chapters seven and eight dealt with *Love* by means of a ramble through romance, sex, and marriage; and chapter nine touched at least tangentially on *Money* as it impinges on vocation. That now leaves us *Health,* which I propose to deal with in an equally oblique chapter on physical well-being. But since well-being in general (happiness, for short) has been our focus all along, I want to cast what I have to say in the form of an observation on the way in which religion, as I've defined it, undermines our happiness—on the way it gums up everything from romance to vocation, from birth to death.

I've already made the point that religion claims to be the one, true, effective cause of well-being. And I've insisted that such a claim is false because the parallel universe in which religion reigns supreme has no necessary or effective connection with the real world in which we stumble along by dumb luck—or more importantly, with the God of the Judeo-Christian revelation who chooses to share that luck with us. But here I want to go further. I'm going to maintain that precisely because religion doesn't work, one of its hallmarks, when it tries to operate in the real world, must inevitably be *secrecy:* it demands that everybody (its adherents as well as the general public) be kept in the dark about the ineffectuality of its methods and results.

The religions of health, money, and love—and of sex, romance, marriage, work, dieting, eating, jogging, or working out—all function as *mystery cults.* They are presented to us as possessing a secret *gnosis,* a private knowledge to be carefully guarded by the elect and to be extended to the general run of humanity only after the most exacting initiation rites. And the reason for all the secrecy is to protect the religions from the profane reality of life—from the vulgar luck which, if allowed even a moment's contact with them, will promptly upset their applecart. Take crash diets, for example. The fact of the matter, of course, is that they are frauds: the only thing that can permanently change anyone's weight is a permanent change in eating and exercise habits. But because that profane reality must not be allowed to intrude upon the religion of dieting, the purveyors of that religion are always pushing some new *gnosis,* some till-now-unrevealed secret that, unlike all the previous secrets, will be the first one to deliver the goods. And for a suitable fee—at the price of the latest book or the most recently touted fat farm—they will initiate you into the latest mystery. To be sure, that one won't work either. But once you have bought the religious principle of crash dieting, it doesn't matter. You have been hooked into the perpetual necessity of being a guardian of mysteries rather than a dealer in facts: therefore you are always fair game, no matter what the facts, for any mystery that comes along next.

Earlier in this book, I made the point that Christianity is not a religion but rather the proclamation that God has gone ahead on his own and ended religion by accomplishing in Jesus, free of charge, whatever it was that religion was trying to do. He has closed the religion shop for good and simply handed over—not to select cultists but to absolutely everybody—all the goods that the shop advertised but never carried. Let me expand on that now in the light of my observation about the *secrecy* of religion.

Christianity, properly understood, has no need whatsoever to guard itself against the profaneness of reality. It is not for some esoteric group of finer types who have glommed onto the latest *gnosis;* rather it proclaims that God in Christ has, quite apart from anybody's *gnosis* or secret recipe, forgiven *all* sinners and raised *all* the dead. It is, in short, not esoteric and fine but catholic and vulgar. And so, far from having to guard its revelation from defilement by the tacky facts of a changing and chancy world, it makes the outrageous claim that the profane world itself is the supreme arena of divine action. Jesus saves the world simply by entering the luck of its ordinary draw on the cross. He dies not as a sacrifice in the temple but as a criminal in the city dump. He suffers not as a religionist but as a convicted anti-religionist—as a blasphemer. Furthermore, in proclaiming that his death is in fact present *in all deaths* (whether those who die know it or not), Christianity offers the world the ultimate profanity: it announces the absurd Good News that the only ticket anyone needs to the new creation is the one ticket everyone has, namely, death. And finally, to cap the vulgarity, it says that no one needs to *do* anything—not rack up any scores, not achieve any level of acceptability, not do any job, secret or public—to cash in on that ticket. We need only to *believe* Jesus when he says the job has been done in his death. All the secret, sacred businesses of religion, you see (the *right* creeds, the *proper* cultic performances, the *appropriate* codes of conduct), go down the drain and give place to the God who, at the bottom of the drain, does the job on anyone who comes along. There isn't a single religious mystery left; just a loud, cosmic laugh at the crazy catholicity of it all.

But enough, perhaps, of that: we are so enamored of religion that almost no one can hear the Good News anyway. Back to the more promising business of pointing out the holes of secrecy in the religions we know and love. Take the religion of sex, for example.

It decrees, first of all, that everybody must have a marvelous sex life. Next, it goes on to specify what it will deign to call marvelous: just how many times a day, week, or month you must "have sex," just how protracted and/or satisfying each episode of it must be, and just how long into your declining years it must be kept up. But finally, the religion of sex does what mystery religions always do: it tells you that if you don't have a marvelous sex life, *it's all your fault* because you don't have the right *gnosis.* And it volunteers to impart that mysterious knowledge by therapy, gadgetry, or conjuring—invariably at a price.

Notice, however, what that does to people. Since it is a fact that very few of us have sex lives that conform to the criteria of the sexual mystery religion, almost none of us admits to the sex life he or she actually has. Not only has the religion tricked us into believing that its *gnosis* might possibly bring us up to snuff; it has also conned us into being ashamed of the below-snuff performances we do have. And why? Because we see ourselves as heretics from the religion of sex. That is why you seldom hear people at dinner parties (loudmouthed sexual acrobats and barefaced bluffers excepted) admit to their sex lives as they actually are. The secrecy of the religion makes *us* secretive as well. Not only do we keep the truth of our performances from others; we keep it from ourselves. But then, with the shame of our true condition thus hidden, we feel free to heap the blame for it on whomever or whatever is handy at the time: "My wife is unresponsive"; "My husband is no lover"; "My mother messed me up"; "I have a headache"; or, "Gee, honey, I need to get my sleep." The secret of the religion of sex, therefore, is safe with us. We can go on believing the twin lies that we didn't fail it and it didn't fail us: our mess is somebody else's fault.

Sex, however, is by no means the only example of secret *gnosis* at work. Consider next the religion of money. Somewhere, very early in our training as devout acolytes of the cult of the dollar, we were taught in no uncertain terms *not to talk* about the mystery. It was blasphemous to ask others how much money they had—and it would incur the wrath of the gods to go around telling others how much *we* were worth. You may want to tell me that such instruction was motivated by simple prudence, but I refuse to believe that. Suppose, for instance, that we both work for the same firm. Our salaries are no secret from the authorities who pay them; yet how unwilling those same authorities are to have us compare notes. It took the entire history of the labor movement to achieve even moderate disclosure of who was getting what; to this day, any outfit that can get away with it will make it as hard as possible to get a true picture of the perks, fringe benefits, and stock options of management.

And the horrendous part of it all is that far from being rebels against it, we are—except for an occasional outburst of inquisitiveness about the secrets of the higher-ups—good little altar boys and girls when it comes to our own secrets. When was the last time you told even a good friend how much money you had in the bank? If there was even a first time, I'd almost be willing to bet you did so not as an apostate from the religion of money but simply as a complainer against the gods. If you were broke, you may have revealed *how little* you had; but if you were flush, you were devoutly careful never to reveal *how much.* In fact, I would go so far as to say that both of us (I am no more a bold heretic about this than you are) invariably have the same true-believer's aversion to any serious apostate from the religion of money we might meet. We will lend a buck to a brother who's short, or give canned goods to strangers who are in a tight spot; but for the embarrassingly poor and the chronically impecunious we have only the fearful disdain we reserve for those who shock our piety. They are the real heretics; and even though we may hide our aversion to them under blankets of prudence or bushels of economic palaver ("you can't solve problems by throwing money at them"), we scrupulously avoid such people like the religion-threatening plague they are. Once again, we reveal ourselves as the guardians of the gnostic flame: rather than question our religion, we blame *them* for not practicing it.

But since this chapter is supposed to be about physical well-being, let us move on to the even sillier things we do to keep the secrets of the religions of health. Sex, at least in our time, is one of the large religious subjects; and money, as it always has been, is the largest of all. The seriousness with which we treat their demands for secrecy, while no less silly than our commitment to hiding our rituals with bath-towel labels or sidewalk cracks, is itself hidden from us by their supposed magnitude. But nowhere more than in the religions of health is the sham of secret solemnity easier to spot—and to blow away with one loud laugh.

Begin with the simple matter of weight. I tip the scales at x pounds, you at y . . .

No. Let me begin again, since I have just fallen into the very secrecy I set out to criticize. I tip the scales at 167 pounds, you at _____ (fill in the blank—honestly). Now then. Those two weights are simply facts about us. They are no more hidden from the world than our peculiar walks, our eye color, our sweet (or sour) breath, or our excesses with the wine bottle. Nevertheless, religion invariably keeps us from admitting that these "secrets" of ours are known. I once weighed in at 230 pounds; but I did all the hiding I thought the cult of slimness required of me. I stopped going to the beach; I disguised my breathiness after three flights of stairs; and with no exceptions (until after I was sure my weight was going down), I avoided the bathroom scale. Yet now, as I look at pictures of my considerable self in that period, it had to have been perfectly obvious that I was fat. My secret was kept only in the parallel universe inside my devout head; in the real world, the truth about me was as plain as day.

Don't get me wrong. I am as happy as anyone would be (middle linebackers excepted) at not weighing 230 anymore. But I'm not at all certain that I'm not still a votary of the religion of weight. To this day, I stay off the scale after the Christmas holidays; and when I weigh myself at other times of the year, it is only after I have run four miles and perspired off the pound or so of fluid I will put right back with my next three glasses of water. Do you see the point? Since I am fooling nobody—not even myself—why am I still so busy hiding? The answer is that I am still trying to conjure with my avoirdupois by the religion of weight, when what I should obviously be doing (preferably for some down-to-earth reason) is eating less and running more.

One last comment before leaving the subject of weight. There was one thing I did enjoy about being fat, and that was the taste of freedom from religion that it gave me. For all those years, even though I bought into the pieties of weight, I was still a bit of a heretic: I ate as much as I wanted of whatever I wanted. My only criterion was: was it good? And that has stood by me. I can honestly say that I have never sworn off anything the mystery cult of thinness told me to avoid. Not butter, not corned beef fat, not heavy cream, not sugar, not wine, not liquor, not gnocchi, pastry, cookies, or cake. If I have eventually come to eat less, I have at least refrained from the reality-hating idiocy of thinking that trimness can only be achieved by eating *less well.* I am still an omnivore: *nihil sapidum alienum a me puto.* And I still condemn no one for the heresy of being fat. As long as they are jolly about it, they're fine by me: *neminem hilarum alienum a me puto,* either.

Which brings us, naturally enough, to the supremely silly religions of food that are now more popular than almost any others. Not that they haven't always enjoyed great vogue. One of the oldest beliefs of the human race—despite the plain, hard fact that people need food to live and can, in reasonable health, digest almost anything that grows, walks, flies, or swims—is that food will kill you unless it is carefully religionized. Cucumbers, it was once believed, had to have their baleful qualities exorcized by slicing off a "heel" and rubbing the cut ends together until they foamed. Eggplants had to be soaked in brine to remove their "poison." Raw vegetables were bad for you and raw meat was certain death. In our days, though, that list has grown beyond belief—or more correctly, beyond anything that could be accounted for *except* by belief. Salt, refined sugar, animal fats; red meat, all meat; hard liquor but not wine, hard liquor *and* wine—all have come under the interdict, along with a host of demons with names like calories, cholesterol, and nitrosamines. People used to say grace before meals and dig in;

now they must sit down and recite the whole nutritional catechism before nibbling at the unsalted, undercooked veggies that are the only doctrinally correct items on the table.

And what is the secret that lurks behind all that flannel-mouthed religiosity? What is the mystery that these devotees of orthodox eating are guarding? It is that there will be a new mystery along next week—and that the adepts of the cult of nutrition will mindlessly but just as noisily embrace it as the final article of faith. Olive oil was once as bad for you as bacon grease because it was demon-possessed by just as many calories. But then it was discovered to be harboring angels called mono-unsaturated fats—and promptly granted admission to the nutritional pantheon. By and by, some food theologian will probably prove that those angels have fallen and turned into demons again. But through all the revisions of the catechism, the true believers will never once doubt the newest revelation, even if it tells them to eat today what would have killed them yesterday.

"But," you say, "isn't it true that the eating habits of most Americans *are* killing them?" My answer is no. People die because the human race is mortal. What they eat may cause them to die sooner (*much* sooner if they eat strychnine; *less* soon perhaps—barring plane crashes—if they eat Hollandaise sauce). But in any case, sometime before they reach the age of a hundred and twenty, they will die; and no religion of eating, however perfectly obeyed, will make the slightest difference in that. Therefore the last secret of the cult of nutrition—the mystery to be guarded at all costs—is that the implicit promise of immortality (which is the principal selling point of the whole religion) is bunk. The idol in the innermost sanctum doesn't just have no clothes on; it isn't even there. But the faithful must scrupulously avoid facing that fact. The one question they must never ask is whether living indefinitely on a diet of tofu and organically grown green leaves—without even salt to perk it up, or wine to wash it down, or a nice smoke to top it off—even vaguely resembles living as the human race in its earthy wisdom has defined it.

That, you see, is the big question. And on that, I am one hundred percent apostate from all the religions of health. I am simply tired of uplift, whether at the table, in the armchair, or anywhere else. I am sick of all the pious types who gasp when they watch me salt a dish on the stove, or put butter and cream into mashed potatoes, or leave a respectable amount of fat on my pork chops when I smother them with onions. I am mortally insulted by snide signs thanking me for not smoking. And I flatly refuse to believe that well-being is in any way furthered by ill-living.

Oh, I know. You want me to qualify all that. You want me to write a paragraph on moderation—or at least a sentence that makes a bow to the religion of health by calling the things I enjoy my "vices," or by referring to my smoke-shrouded end of the dinner table as "the sinners' corner." But I won't. A moderate life, to me, is about as exciting as a moderate love affair, or a moderate marriage, or a moderate banana split. I want a terrific life. So you write the paragraph yourself and let me get on with my immoderate pursuit of happiness.

The net result of the religions of food is noncooking, non-dining, and nonliving. Consider restaurants. The dishes now served in most public places come to the table unfinished: in deference to the cultists, the all-important salt—the judicious salinity that brings all the flavors together—is missing. Or consider domestic dining. The barely cooked, totally uncut green beans that hostesses currently plunk in front of you are a threat: I have a vision of getting one stuck crosswise in my mouth and living the rest of my life with my cheeks propped out by a beanstick. And for a final horror, consider the smokeless, drinkless "life" proposed by the guardians of the mystery of health: it is nothing less than death by drabness.

Oh once again, I know. After that last sentence you want another qualification. You would like a few words about alco-holism, perhaps—about the fact that some people, unfortunately, are allergic to certain things and would be wise to avoid them altogether. Well of course they would. So you write those words too if you like—even though the press is already filled to the brim with them. For myself, I am too busy trying to demolish an entire religion—whose false doctrines, incidentally, the press conspires never to mention.

One last thing about food before moving on. It is a feature of the current press to berate as heretical the junk-food diet on which many Americans subsist: salty french fries, fatty burgers, chocolate chip cookies, and diet soft drinks. But I am a happy heretic about that as well. To be sure, I can criticize such a diet as roundly as anyone. The french fries are usually limp, the burgers mediocre, the cookies full of imitation vanilla, and the drinks devoid of the sugar I love. But beneath all the trashy eating there is a kind of rough-and-ready protestantism, a rumbling of revolt among the peasants against the high-flown medievalism of the food cultists—a breath of sanity, if you will, that blows away the myths of salt, fat, and sugar and proclaims the unwillingness of the great unwashed to be conned out of taste by mumbo jumbo. The protestantism is not pure, of course: the diet soda in the list I just gave you is a vestige of unreformed religion that should have been tossed out with all the other superstitions. But the junk-food revolution is quite protestant enough to give me hope that despite their present tyranny, the mysteries of the nutrition church will some day be seen as the transparent lies they are—and that taste, now so long banished, will once again be restored to our tables.

My final illustration of the religion of health as the enemy of the well-being it professes to enhance is the cult of exercise. Since I play at no sports, ply no weights, and plunk down no dollars for ski machines, I confine my remarks to the one exercise I know something about: running. Though you may be tired of hearing about my personal apostasies by now, I am a heretic from the religion of jogging, too. I have pounded the roads for almost thirty years but I have never worn a running suit, clocked myself, competed in races, joined a jogging class, or in any way tried to achieve religious respectability by improving my style or my performance. I run year-round and in all weather—and on pavement, not tracks. I wear old clothes: ratty paint pants in the summer and varying numbers of pairs of slacks in the winter (it took me a good many years to work my way down from 230 pounds, so I have plenty of 36s, 40s, and 44s to layer up nicely). I carry a stick, not a jogger's aerosol can, for dealing with loose dogs; and until the deer ticks decided to infect the east coast with Lyme disease, I used to lie down on the ground in the middle of my run and watch the clouds go by. I do, admittedly, wear running shoes (nobody's protestantism is perfect), but at least I refuse to read the ever-increasing wads of mystic hype that come with each new pair.

And what is my reward for all that? The plain pleasures of running: breathing the air, feeling the sun, rain, wind, and snow on my face, and enjoying the mindlessness that sheer physical repetitiveness can bring. In short, my reward is feeling human and being in the real world, if only for an hour a day. It is not status, or cachet, or self-improvement. If I am thinner than I once was, that is nice. But since, as my friends assure me, I'm not noticeably better, that is equally nice: it proves I'm no pushover for uplift. If the day ever comes when I can't run, I shall walk. When I can't walk, I shall sit in a chair and smell the wind. And when I can't sit up any more, I shall lie on my back and watch the clouds once again. But I will not do any of it for reasons of religion—only because it pleases *me*.

Our well-being cannot be furthered by pasting a religious bumper sticker on down-to-earth activities: their own glory is quite enough to make us happy. The make-believe just makes us sad, or mad, or both.

11

Postscript

FOR SOME TIME NOW (IF NOT FROM THE VERY START OF THIS book), I have heard an objection forming in your mind. My insistence that God has chosen to make luck and not intervention his normal device for running the world and establishing his relationship with us has raised three large questions—or better said, perhaps, one major question and two corollaries to it. Accordingly, as we head for the barn on the subjects of Health, Money, and Love, let me try to offer some conciliatory responses to your concerns.

Your first question is: Isn't luck, or chance, rather a casual or even an uncaring way for a supposedly respectable God to pursue his relationship with creation? If God is all-knowing and all-powerful—and to raise the main point, if he is all-loving and all-good— shouldn't we expect him to have a much more beneficent finger in the world's pie than I have suggested? If we, with all our limitations, can intervene regularly to rescue our loved ones from bad luck (pulling out a child who falls in the fireplace, bandaging cuts, kissing boo-boos), why shouldn't God be at least as considerate and helpful?

Your second question follows logically from that. If God (as I have maintained) is *not* better than we are—if in fact he seems worse and only rarely intervenes with the help we so frequently need—doesn't that lead straight to indifference, inaction, or even despair on our part? If his prevailing attitude toward our lives is *che sarà, sarà*—if he insists that our bad luck is every bit as much the vehicle of his relationship with us as our good luck—doesn't that tend to discourage us from *caring* much about anything? Doesn't it lead, in short, to quietism or even fatalism?

And your last question is yet another corollary to all of the above: if it's true that *any* luck that befalls us is his idea of a proper rendezvous for a divine Lover, why should we *pray*—why should we ask for more comfortable or more mannerly assignations from him? If he is so alarmingly like a slot machine, a one-armed bandit that simply treats us to whatever happens to turn up by chance—and if he, as the casino owner, is content to make only the most occasional exceptions to the laws of chance—what reason have we to expect that telling him about our needs or our comfort can in any way influence him to be more accommodating to us?

So much for the questions. If I have not covered all the objections in your mind I have at least, by stating them as baldly as possible, not fudged the ones I did mention in favor of my own ideas. On then with the answers, such as they may be.

As I see it, the problem that underlies your first question (Why would a respectable God prefer luck to intervention when it comes to running the world?) is our reluctance to admit that the God of the Judeo-Christian revelation—not to mention the God of ordinary historical experience—is *not* a respectable God. Both Scripture and history make it quite plain that despite all the human race's efforts to write up the requirements for membership in the Good God Club, God himself has simply declined to join. Contrary to what we think he ought to be doing, he makes his sun to shine on the evil and on the good and sends rain on the just and the unjust. Despite our predilections, murderers regularly get away with murder, liars with lying, destroyers with destruction, and sinners in general with whatever sinning they happen to be fond of. Theologians, of course, have felt free to tell God that he ought to be running a tighter ship; but God steers almost entirely by luck, and that is that. The tight ship of the respectable God sails only in the parallel universe of religion. In the real world, heading for the rocks is every bit as much a part of God's navigation as plain sailing.

And lest we should be tempted to look in Scripture for some contradiction of this divine haphazardness, he has displayed on its pages proof after proof of the divine recklessness. Israel's history is a history of calamity: God's chosen nation; century after century, gets run over by every steamrolling superpower in the ancient world. Moreover, lest we should try to find exceptions to this pre-dilection for luck over intervention in God's dealing with *individuals* in Scripture, he makes it clear that he interferes no more with their personal calamities than with those of the nation. Abraham, Jacob, Moses, Jeremiah, Jesus—all of them meet God more signif-icantly in the dark luck of their several draws than in the odd godsend, however spellbinding. His occasional jimmyings of their histories are only the *signs* of his program for their lives; they are not the program itself. Because that program is something quite distinct from any sign: it is the establishment and pursuit of a mysterious relationship with them in the changing and chancy happenings of their actual history. Much as we may dislike it—however little we may think of his indiscriminate willingness to let our lives carom from beneficent pillar to calamitous post—he no more keeps us in the best of times than he rescues us from the worst. Rather he tells us only that he will be with us in both—and that in fact, when push comes to shove, he has a bizarre preference for calamity. The world is saved *on* the cross, not *from* it.

So the answer to the other part of your first question (Isn't the God of luck actually *worse* than we are—more cruel, less caring?) is yes, it certainly looks that way. God *is* unfair by our standards. He *does* seem indifferent. And sprinkled through the pages of Scripture—like the salt that seasons, balances, and perfects the whole dish of revelation—is the witness of the tormented, fact-facing few who had the nerve to stand up to God and say as much. From Isaiah's "How long, O Lord?" to Job's "Why did I not die at birth?" to Jesus' "My God, my God, why have you forsaken me?" there goes up the complaint that sees, better than any mousy acceptance of theological soft soap, how God really works. And it sees that reality because it comes from the hearts of those who love God more than their own ideas about him—from those who would rather have *him* in his distasteful truth than all the consolations of theology.

Do you see? The ultimate answer to all of your first question is that there is no answer except the promised presence of God *in all luck.* And the only thing you can do with that answer is decide to trust the promise. However bad God's manners as a lover may be, however much we may complain that his standards for the conduct of a love affair are lower than ours for lunch with an enemy, he is the only lover we have—and if we talk ourselves into objecting to his manners, we talk ourselves out of the only love there really is. I wish I could tell you something more pleasant than that, but I can't. For your comfort, though, I think it's fair to say that God's insistence on being with us *in* our disasters rather than fishing us out of them also shows him to be *at least as good* as we are. Rescue from disaster has never been the best we had to offer those who suffer. As often as not, it isn't even something we're able to offer. For the permanently crippled, the hopelessly bereaved, or the terminally ill, the only gift we have to give is our presence in love; and while that's not what they might have asked for, it certainly is ourselves at our best. Why God couldn't manage to be a bit better than our best, I don't know. All I know is that at least he's honest enough never finally to have told us he *was* better than that. It isn't much, I admit; but if you can bring yourself to accept it, it will give you a lot fewer problems than the nice, dishonest God of the armchair theologians who got us into this problem to begin with.

Which brings me to the second of your questions: Doesn't a

world run almost entirely by luck constitute a temptation to quietism, fatalism, or even despair? Doesn't it lead to the conclusion that there's no use doing anything because, by God's design, what will be, will be, and no action on our part can stop it?

My answer is no; but to understand why, you have to examine a sleeper—a false, hidden assumption—in the formulation of your question. When people talk about luck or chance, they almost always imagine it as a *causal* phenomenon, a determinative force that makes things happen the way they do. Commonly, of course, this leads them straight into religion—into the search for some system that will clue them in to the way the phenomenon operates and so enable them to control it, or at least take advantage of it. But since I have already ruled out religion as a useful option for living in a chancy world—indeed, since it is precisely my proscribing of religion that has made you feel so helpless, and therefore so loath to accept luck as God's way of running the universe—I'm not going to say anything more about it here. Instead, I want you to look at how chance actually operates.

Chance, properly understood, never *causes* anything to happen; rather, it is a description of how the assorted causes of events vary in certain instances. Take the tossing of a coin, for example. We all know that if you flip a penny into the air and let it fall to the ground, it will land either heads up, tails up, or (so rarely as to be a negligible possibility) on its edge. But we also know two more things. The first is that if you flip the penny just once, you "take your chances" as to whether it will come down heads or tails: so much so that we use the single toss as a tried and true way of deciding things impartially—that is, independently of the wishes or influences of those involved in the decision. But the second thing we know is that if you flip the penny ten million times, it will land heads up very close to five million times and tails up very close to the same figure—so close, in fact, that we even use the phrase "the laws of chance" to describe this second phenomenon.

Notice, however, that whatever those "laws" may be, they have no causal effect on any particular event. The reason why, on a given toss, the penny lands the way it does is simply the interaction of the various causes involved in that toss: you started out, let us say, by balancing it (heads or tails up) on your fingernail; you propelled it upwards with a certain definite force; it turned in the air (against the air's resistance) just so many times before it reached the zenith of the toss; on descending, it turned just so many more times before it reached the ground; it bounced or it did not; and then it came to rest, displaying whichever side was up at the end of the process. The "laws" of chance, you see, did not cause a single event in the toss; they only describe how the causes will vary if you make a sufficiently high number of tosses. In fact, if you could manage to rig all the causative factors so that they were identical in each toss (same thumb force, same air resistance, same speed of turning, same zenith, same ground level, same angle of impact), you could guarantee yourself ten million instances in a row of heads (or tails) up.

Do you see the point? Since *you* are one of the factors—one of the varying causes—in any chance event you choose to involve yourself with, there is no reason for you to come to the conclusion that chance or luck implies fatalistic determinism. Even if you choose *not* to involve yourself with a particular chance event, that choice itself becomes part of the process. There is an old story about Moishe, the janitor of a synagogue, who prayed every day that God would arrange for him to win the lottery. After many months, he finally went to the Rabbi and complained that God either did not exist or was ignoring his prayers. The Rabbi, however, was busy and got rid of Moishe by telling him simply to go back into the synagogue and pray again. Moishe did just that: "O God!" he said. "You must have heard my prayers; why won't you help me? I have served you well. What more must I do?" And suddenly, from the roof of the synagogue, came a voice from heaven: "Moishe! Give us a break! Buy a ticket!"

It is entirely possible, of course—indeed, given the odds, it is practically a sure thing—that almost every ticket buyer will *not* win the lottery. But since it is absolutely certain that no nonbuyer will ever win it, Moishe had no grounds for fatalism—and neither do we. Both he and we are part of the causative process. We may be a small part—so small that the chances of our coming out on top of the process are almost zero. But we are still contributors to it—causes within it—and the process, once we have made our contribution, is not quite what it would have been without us.

So we are back at what I said earlier. In a world run by luck, the call of God is not a call into the following of some plan that will guarantee a life drawn up to either our or God's specifications. It is simply a call into the *next thing* we choose to do or not to do, as the case may be. It is a call to the *next step* in the dance of a free creation; and whatever we do about that next step—whether we take it brilliantly, or disastrously, or not at all—the dance will always be different as a result of what we did. Even if our next step consists of nothing more than an acceptance of being trampled to death by the other dancers, it still affects the dance. As a matter of fact, when God in Jesus finally reveals his chosen method for reconciling the Dance of Creation, it turns out to be precisely an acceptance of being trampled to death by others: he embraces the worst of luck on the cross and pronounces the whole job done. The acceptance of luck, therefore, is anything but quietism or fatalism. It is the joining of a dance that has been made glorious by God's joining of it. It is the finding—in all partners, and in the moves of all partners—of the Only Partner who ever claimed to redeem the dance without interfering with it.

And that, nicely enough, brings us to your third question: Why bother to pray if God's almost universal method of operation is simply chance—simply an acceptance of whatever the various dancers decide to contribute as *their thing?* Why ask for deliverance from cancer when God is cheering for the cancer cells every bit as much as he is cheering for you? Why ask for anything—health, money, or love—if God smiles equally on their presence or their absence from your life?

The first answer is the example of Jesus in the Garden of Gethsemane. After months of saying that the whole purpose of his ministry was to die, he prays on the night before his death that if it be possible, "this cup might pass" from him—that the whole business might be called off. And why does he do that? Because that's what he felt like asking for at that moment; because, as one of the free, causative agents of creation, that's the next step *he,* as the human, feeling, fearful being he is, would like to take; because that's what he wants there and then. But if he, as God incarnate, can make such a request—if he can poke into the dance even such a refusal of the dance as that—then the dance is a lot more accommodating than the strictures of anybody's theology (even Jesus') might have led us to believe. If he can pray not to die, then there is no such thing as unworthy prayer or inappropriate prayer; there is only prayer—only whatever comes out of our minds and hearts, no questions asked. We can ask to be made model citizens or spiritual giants. We can ask to be cured of cancer, hangnails, bad breath, or having two left feet. We can ask that we find our long-lost love or our recently misplaced car keys. In prayer, as in life, we can take *any next step* we choose because the God who works in all luck *presides* in all luck.

In all honesty, though, that first answer only brings us to the heart of your question, which is: Why pray, when God—even in Jesus' case—is obviously so much fonder of letting luck run its course than of jimmying it in our favor? Why ask for anything in particular when everything in general seems to be so indiscriminately acceptable to him? But just as there was a sleeper in your second question (Why *do* anything?) so there is a sleeper in this one. Just as you forgot that no matter what you did or didn't do, you still had an effect (small or great) on the Dance of Creation, so here you have forgotten that what God is up to in "running the world by luck" is not the management of some machine called the universe but the establishment and fulfillment of his *relationship* with every single thing in creation.

For Christians at least, God is neither a plant manager nor a machine minder; he is rather, *Daddy.* When Jesus taught his disciples to pray, he had them address God as *Abba,* Father—and he seems, moreover, to have used the word "father" in its diminutive, familiar form. Therefore, if any image in the Lord's prayer presents itself to us as governing it is an intimate, parental image, not an abstract, theological one. So when you ask the question, Why pray?, you should set aside all the philosophical claptrap about what you should ask for in your prayers or how God should answer them and confine yourself to exploring the parental imagery. Watch what happens when you do.

Somewhere, back in the dim recesses of my Christian upbringing, someone told me that God had three answers to prayer: yes, no, and wait. But however well-intentioned that instruction was—it was no doubt meant to give me hope that when a yes to my requests was not immediately forthcoming, I might read God's notorious silence as a mysterious deferral of his compliance to some even better time—I never thought much of it. It seemed simply disingenuous. Lately, though, as I have reflected on the image of God as Daddy and listened carefully to the answers parents actually give to their children's requests, I have finally seen what was wrong with it. There are still, of course, three answers; but they are not yes, no, and wait. They are in fact, yes, no, and *we'll see*—with "we'll see" (as any child will attest) by far the commonest answer.

You will tell me, of course, that "we'll see" is just a subterfuge parents use to avoid saying "no" on the spot. But my children long ago came to that cynical conclusion and I think no more of it from your lips than I did from theirs. Admittedly, the answer is used that way; but just because a truth can be abused doesn't mean that it can't still be true. So far from being willing to write off "we'll see" as a cop-out, I am disposed to see what can be made of it in terms of our relationship to God in prayer.

Think the phrase through. When parents use it at their best, it actually means something like, "Yes, Johnny, I know you want a rifle now; but let's both of us see how that desire works out in our lives." Sometimes, of course, we simply mean that we just don't know, or haven't worked out, the implications of giving him a rifle. But at other times we say "we'll see" because while we do indeed know those implications, there is no way at present of our communicating them to Johnny's understanding: we really will have to see if and when he can grasp them.

Next, therefore, transfer the parental imagery to God. Abstract theology, to be sure, will tell you that my first suggestion as to what "we'll see" might mean cannot apply to God: God is supposed to know everything, perfectly, at all times. I could argue with that. The God of Scripture seems not to have read the theologians' books: for someone who supposedly knows in advance all about his people's backsliding, for example, he still gets surprisingly exercised when he comes across specific instances of it. But let that pass. The second meaning of "we'll see" (namely, that *we* know the implications of the request but the child is not ready to understand them) can certainly apply to God—even to the God of the theologians. Because even if God does know everything his creatures ever did or will do, he knows those things—past, present, and future—*simultaneously:* he knows them, in other words, by an *eternal, timeless watching* of what his creatures, in time, do with their freedom. However, because we know past, present, and future only *sequentially,* there is no way (short of his giving us the false impression that tomorrow is outside the realm of luck and already set in cement just like yesterday) that he can say anything but "we'll see" to most of our requests (including, if you think about it, even Jesus' request in Gethsemane). And he is limited to that answer not because he is waiting for our knowledge to catch up with his but because *we* have to wait for the appropriate time to do, by the luck of the draw, whatever we in our freedom are going to offer him for his knowing.

Naturally, all of this knowledge-chopping raises the problem of God's foreknowledge of the future. But the problem lies almost entirely in a misunderstanding. Strictly speaking, God doesn't *foreknow* anything; he just knows everything *at once.* His knowledge of the future, in other words, is like our knowledge of the past. For me, the events of last Monday, Tuesday, and Wednesday are now known simultaneously: while I can run through

them in memory in the sequence in which they happened historically, I can also entertain them in any other sequence I like. But as
I sit myself down mentally in last Monday, for example, and think
of what I did on the following Wednesday, I in no way lose sight
of the fact that my actions on Wednesday were every bit as freely
chosen as my actions on Monday. *Foreknowledge,* at least in this
instance, has nothing to do with *predeterminism.* Foreknowledge, in
fact, is strictly a human category. So the right way to talk about
God's knowledge of the future is to pattern our discourse about it
on our knowledge of the past: that is, to play with the tenses a bit
and say that *God knows what I did **tomorrow**.* And even in his
eternity, he knows what I *did tomorrow* in exactly the same way as I
know it temporally when tomorrow arrives: we both see exactly and
only how the luck of our mutual draw works out. We both *find out*
the moves of the dance by which he calls us into relationship with
himself.

If you like, I shall apologize for that excursion into theology. But not abjectly, because it has brought us back to the main
point to be made about prayer—or any other action on our part.
God says "we'll see" to most of our earnest requests and bright
ideas because he really means it. "You and I," he says to each of
us, "—you and I in our relationship, in the mutual dance of luck
which is my ultimate call to you—you and I will see how *our* luck
works out in all the next things. We'll see it *together* as we did on
the cross where I, as the proprietor of the only hundred percent
honest casino anywhere, always make a profit for both of us. I
invented luck, and I'm in it with you. So whether you pray or
don't pray, whether you act or don't act, our relationship is still
there—and ultimately that's all that counts.

"But if you can manage it," God adds, "it will be a whole lot
more fun if we can keep the conversation going."

12

Epilogue

A WHILE BACK, WHEN I WAS APOLOGIZING FOR GOD'S PERSIS-
tent nonintervention in the calamities of the world, I offered you
the admittedly modest consolation that he is at least honest enough
never finally to have claimed that he was better than we are when
it comes to delivering help. The best he seems willing to do in
desperate cases is remarkably like the best we can do: namely, to be
personally, if helplessly, present out of love and let the changes and
chances of this mortal life roll on. Now though, at the end of this
book, I want to give you one more reassurance. Not only is he honest
enough not to claim he helps when he doesn't; he is also decent
enough to feel bad about the divine neglect.

In the eleventh chapter of the Gospel according to John,
Jesus comes to Bethany, the village where Mary and her sister
Martha are mourning the death of their brother Lazarus. Jesus was
not present when Lazarus took sick; and even though he received
word of his friend's illness, he purposely stayed away until he was
sure Lazarus was dead. Naturally enough, both Martha and Mary

had hoped that Jesus would come and heal their brother: in fact, each of the sisters' first words of greeting to him were, "Lord, if you had been here, my brother would not have died." Jesus, however, insists that Lazarus will rise again. And Martha, drawing on her childhood training (presumably by the Pharisees), says, "Yes, I know: he will rise again in the resurrection at the last day." But then Jesus says a strange thing to her. "No," he says in effect. "*I am the resurrection and the life.*" *His very presence,* in other words, is the resurrection: her brother will live because Jesus is his life here and now. And so it happens—but only after something peculiar.

Before Jesus actually commands Lazarus to come forth from the tomb, the Gospel writer records (in the shortest verse in all of Scripture, John 11:35) that "Jesus wept." The crowd surrounding him found his tears bizarre at the time and we find them bizarre still. We even have the same objection: "Couldn't this person who opened the eyes of the blind have arranged things so that this man wouldn't have died?" But Jesus simply ignores the theological challenge and does something even more bizarre: he approaches the tomb, John says, *embrimómenos en heautô—*"groaning with *upsetment* [or even *anger*] in himself."

There have, of course, been facile explanations of his troubled mentality at the door of the tomb: he was angry at the crowd's unbelief, perhaps, or he had second thoughts about his decision to stay away. But since none of those will hold up in the context, my explanation is different. The verb *embrimásthai* is used several times in the New Testament to describe Jesus' state of mind when he helped people by doing miracles: in Matthew 9:30, when he heals two blind men; in Mark 1:43, when he heals a leper; and twice in John 11, when he raises Lazarus. It seems to me, therefore, that the interpretation it invites is that Jesus is upset precisely by *the doing of miracles at all—*by the act of offering miraculous band-aids to a world that can only be saved by much more mysterious and radical action. Accordingly, I think that Jesus' disturbed state when he did these patchwork miracles as *signs* of his program sprang from his awareness that his *radical, ultimate* program would not involve patchwork miracles at all but rather an acceptance on the cross of the luck of the world's draw as his chosen way of relating himself to us.

Think only of Lazarus and of what Jesus almost certainly knew about him. Lazarus would indeed rise from the dead, but only to die again some other day—and that time, for good. But even before Lazarus died the second time, he would be the object of a plot by the authorities (see John 12:10) to kill him because he, right along with Jesus, had become a threat to peace and tranquillity. Do you see? Having chosen the luck of the draw as the arena of his ultimate work, he realized that just as he had left Lazarus in the lurch for the rest of his life, so he was leaving the whole world in the lurch for the rest of its history. He realized that while his miracles were effective enough to give people the idea that he was promising them everything, his mysterious, hands-off method of making good on that promise would be indistinguishable from delivering nothing. And so, realizing the rivers of tears that a creation thus left to luck would pour forth, he had the decency to weep himself.

Jesus wept, in other words, at the divine incompetence, at the divine complicity in the nightmare that is history. Someone once said, in a moment of theological extravagance, "The Carpenter of Nazareth made the world." But Jesus weeps because the Carpenter of Nazareth turns out to be a wood-butcher whose sloppy workmanship has so far cost the world two thousand years' worth of misery. He does not come when he is needed; and if he does show up, it is only to fix the bathroom door, not to shore up the subsiding foundation which is the real problem with the house. Even when he comes with miraculous help, therefore, he comes only to plane Lazarus's life, if you will, into an even more cockeyed shape than it had before, not to repair the tilted world that necessitated such a shape to begin with.

And yet . . . and yet. In the strangest way, that is almost more of a consolation than anything else. Had he come among us resolutely committed to being Mr. Goodplane, the Home Repair

Specialist, he would have had to demolish the world in order to save it. By the time he had rebuilt our foundation, and replaced our framing, and reshingled our outside, and replastered our interior, we simply wouldn't be the same house. So he opts instead for the mystery of suffering: he joins his tears with ours at our dilapidation and just moves in and lives with us as we are. He is not the slick, professional god of the theological hucksters; he is the Amateur God who loves every board in the old place, and whose answer to all requests to repair the hell out of it is, "Now, now; we'll see." He is the Lover who is with us in all luck—and who, at the roots of the being he will not tamper with, calls us back to the Love from which we sprang.